Jocelyn—

You already are
Stadium Status!

Best, John

Praise for

STADIUM STATUS

and JOHN BRUBAKER

"I've spent my life in stadiums, I can enthusiastically endorse Coach Bru's new book. It absolutely is *Stadium Status* advice."

—Blake Anderson, Head Football Coach,
Arkansas State University

"I've loved Coach Bru's writing ever since we adapted his book *Seeds of Success* into a screenplay for a major motion picture. Now, I'm completely blown away by *Stadium Status*."

—Bob Burris, Hollywood Producer and Director

"John's book *Stadium Status* gives you insight into the strategies of all sorts of high performers who call the stadium their office. Read it and I'm confident your brand will soar to new heights."

—Lyle Overbay, former Major League Baseball player

"Coach Bru is one of our favorite guests to have on our show. His conversations with us are always incredibly valuable and compelling. His message in *Stadium Status* will forever change how you look at your business. You'll love this book."

—Angel Tuccy and Eric Reamer, Hosts of the nationally
syndicated Experience Pros Radio Show

"In *Stadium Status*, Coach Bru carries us past our threshold of ordinary leadership performance strategies. He challenges our assumptions with gifted insights and a mindset that can make us what Coach is in *HIS* work – a game changer."

—Ken Mannie, MS, MSCC, Head Strength/Conditioning
coach, Michigan State University

"Pick up a copy of Coach Bru's new book, *Stadium Status*, and I promise you'll find some amazing ideas that you can put to action right away to enhance your brand and create raving fans for life."

—Tyler Smith, Manager, Granger Smith & Earl Dibbles Jr.

"A brilliant piece of work! Coach Bru was able to weave amazing parallels between the music industry and entrepreneurship and turn it into a compelling read that I have recommended to all of my colleagues."

—Ryan Vaughn, General Manager,
Anderson Bean Boot Company

"*Stadium Status* is a great read for entrepreneurs, entertainers, or anyone else looking to elevate their business or career. It's packed with great advice from Coach Bru that will inspire anyone driven to succeed."

−Brittany Hodak, Co-Founder at ZinePak

"I wish this book was around when I began my career."

−Jesse Lakes, CEO/Co-Founder, Genius Link

"*Stadium Status* is the most important book on entrepreneurship to come out this year."

−Jeff Schattner, Founder & CEO,
Lawrence Hunt Fashion Inc.

"You hold in your hands 150+ pages of jet fuel to sky rocket your results. I should know, John Brubaker is my coach and I use his strategies every day in my businesses."

−Nate Wadsworth, Real Estate Investor and Representative:
Maine House of Representatives

"If you like country music, and business success you'll love *Stadium Status*."

−Christy "Sweet Tea" Andrulonis, Director of Fun and
Program Director, Colonial Media + Entertainment

"I can't remember the last time I had this much fun reading a "business book". *Stadium Status* is brilliant, inspirational and entertaining."

−Jason Novetsky, Ph.D., Sport Psychology Coach,
Champion Mindset Group

"*Stadium Status* is pure brilliance. Coach Bru is one of the great voices of our time. He's too young to be this smart and talented. I wish I were him."

−Cliff Fazzolari, Award-Winning Author of *Oh Brother!*
The Life & Times of Jeff Fazzolari

"*Stadium Status* is almost as good as the book Coach Bru wrote about me. Almost."

−Coach Morgan Randall, Coaching Icon and
Legend, Radnor University

"Drawing on his own experiences and observations, John lays out an actionable plan for how to develop your own brand. Fun to read and valuable for entrepreneurs of all industries hungry to level up their game."

−Shannon Moss, President and
Founder of Code Gratitude Inc.

STADIUM
STATUS

STADIUM STATUS

Taking Your Business to the Big Time

JOHN BRUBAKER

bibliomotion
inc.

First edition published in 2017
by Bibliomotion, Inc.
711 Third Avenue New York, NY 10017, USA
2 Park Square, Milton Park, Abingdon, Oxon OX14 4RN, UK

© 2017 by Taylor & Francis Group, LLC

Bibliomotion is an imprint of Taylor & Francis Group, an informa business

No claim to original U.S. Government works

Printed on acid-free paper

International Standard Book Number-13: 978-1-138-63669-9 (Hardback)

International Standard eBook Number-13: 978-1-3151-9671-8 (eBook)

Library of Congress Cataloging-in-Publication Data
A catalog record for this book has been requested

Visit the Taylor & Francis Web site at
http://www.taylorandfrancis.com

Printed and bound in the United States of America by Sheridan Books, Inc. (a Sheridan Group Company).

Contents

Acknowledgments

The genesis of the idea for this book belongs to my daughter Meredith. Since before our children were born, my wife and I would play music and read to them at bedtime, and it's a tradition we've continued throughout their childhood. Meredith is definitely her father's daughter. She loves two things: sports and country music. When she turned ten we would listen to our favorite artists on Pandora and read books together on her iPad. One night we ran out of reading material so she began to read the "about the artist" bios on the Pandora stream. Each in its own way, the bios read like every great story, with relatable characters, struggles and setbacks, and ultimately success. After reading a couple of them she suggested I write my next book on business lessons people could learn from country musicians. She has even served as my research assistant on this project.

It's said that as parents we learn more from our children than they do from us. The statement couldn't be more accurate in this case. As she nears adolescence, that challenging age where kids begin to pull away from their parents, our shared love of country music and the fascinating stories of the artists provide us with something we can still enjoy together. So Nashville, we owe you a collective thank you.

A special thank you goes to country music star Granger Smith and his manager Tyler Smith for the inspiration behind the title *Stadium Status*. Granger and his brother Tyler set their sights on achieving stadium status, and to keep their vision top of mind, any time they had a new idea, reached a new milestone, or grew their brand to the next level they'd sign their text and e-mails to each other with #StadiumStatus. You often see the same hashtag at the end of their announcements on social media. These two stadium status performers have been significant influences on my work.

Great teams have great teammates, high fives to Erika Heilman and her team at Bibliomotion as well as Michael Sinocchi, Iris Hsieh, Jonathan Mack and the entire Taylor & Francis team.

Louis Brandeis said it best when he said "There is no great writing, only great re-writing". A very special thank you to Susan Lauzau. You are the most stadium status editor an author could ever ask for.

Foreword

If you're a country music fan, you can probably guess why I'm writing the foreword to *Stadium Status*. Since starting my professional career as an entertainer in 2004, I've taken a unique approach to building a stadium status brand.

You and I are more alike than you may think. We're both in incredibly cutthroat businesses and the margin for error is razor thin. Being an entertainer and being an entrepreneur are more similar than they are different. I should know, I've done both. I've worked as a human resource consultant and am completing my MBA. I've also been a part of ESPN's *College Gameday* intro video since 2006, have served as co-host of USA Network's *Nashville Star* and performed on ABC's *Dancing With the Stars*.

I don't share all that to impress you, I share it to impress upon you that there's no such thing as an overnight success. I didn't just wake up one morning, put on a cowboy hat, and get gigs on TV and rapping on a country album. You don't do something for fifteen years on a lark. What you really need to remember, as you read this, is there is no substitute for hard work and diligence. There is no magic wand to wave to get results, but there is a fast track to better results and Coach Bru provides you with the road map to success in this, his latest book.

Most forewords tell you about the book you're about to read, but this isn't most forewords and this sure isn't like most books. So instead of telling you about the book you're going to read, I'd rather tell you precisely why you should zero in on what Coach Bru has to say in his book.

Coach Bru and I relate to one another so well because I've challenged the conventional thinking of what country music is, and he's done the same as an author and coach. One of my mottos is that innovation is a tradition, not a trend or secondary option . . . authenticity comes in the commitment. That phrase also perfectly describes *Stadium Status*. It's innovative; the concepts you're about to read won't be found in the pages of any other book (or anywhere else, for that matter). In writing it, Coach Bru made a commitment to open up his playbook to you, so to speak. As a result, he speaks from a place of authenticity and shares battle-tested strategies. There are no trendy or flavor-of-the-month ideas in here, for sure.

The difference between this book and other business books is that Coach Bru takes his concept and demonstrates it with concrete examples by stadium status performers, himself, and, in some cases, his clients. There's a real art to taking complex concepts and making them simple to understand in the eyes of the learner. Whether it's in his speaking, coaching, consulting, or in writing this book, Coach Bru demonstrates that he has mastered that art—and you get to reap the benefits.

My music is the intersection between two genres, country and hip-hop; I call it Hick Hop™. While I was the first Hick Hop artist, trademarked the term, and invented an entire genre, there are now many others vying for space in the genre. My wife, Laura, put it very well when she said, "You're not just ahead of the curve, you set the curve and everyone else followed." It's probably why *Stadium Status* resonates so deeply with me. Coach Bru's work is the intersection between the stadium and business, it's his Hick Hop, if you will, and with this book he has indeed set the curve.

Don't let the title mislead you into thinking that these ideas only apply to those who call the stadium their office. You'll also find lots of great examples of companies and small businesses that demonstrate that these *Stadium Status* concepts work in all industries. The book is packed with innovative ideas that I believe will take your brand to new heights, ideas like how to create customers for life using the worst seat in the house and why your audience needs seven different ways to connect to your brand. This book will challenge you and everyone in your company to look at your brand and the way you operate through a different lens. And that's the point: in order to achieve a level of success that will be remembered, you have to be willing to try unique approaches to common problems. Look for unconventional ways to resolve a situation. Looking at problems and situations from different angles can provide you with new and exciting results.

It's not often that I find a book that's equal parts motivation and strategy. But that's exactly what *Stadium Status* is. As I read it I found myself inspired to reexamine my business and some of my ways of thinking. With its easy-to-follow format, you'll feel like Coach Bru is giving you instantly actionable advice as you progress through the chapters.

I strongly recommend you read this book before your competition does.

Troy Coleman
www.CowboyTroy.com

Introduction

Stadium Status: To be a big enough star that you could fill an entire stadium when performing a concert, you know you're big once you've achieved Stadium Status.

—UrbanDictionary.com

That scholarly journal, *Urban Dictionary*, defines stadium status very succinctly: essentially, it means that if you've achieved stadium status you are a big star. Stadium status is, on some level, a goal that lives within every artist, entertainer, and entrepreneur. I know it's the goal that has motivated and driven me in each of my careers.

big time: much more than usual, to the max. The top of the game in whatever game you choose to play.

The great American philosophers at *Urban Dictionary* really nail this one too. Growth that takes you to the point where you reach the highest level (aka the big time) in your industry or market is the goal I hear most entrepreneurs say they are striving for. That stands to reason; we all have a desire to be known and to attract fans to ourselves and our brands, don't we?

What This Book Isn't

This isn't your normal "business book"; as a matter of fact, there's probably nothing normal about it. It's weird by comparison, and I'm proud of that because, as you are about to learn, weird wins. You won't see me quoting management theorists or citing research from journals, white papers, or reports. There isn't a bar graph or a pie chart to be found, and you aren't going to read any boring case studies. There's enough of that out there already. This isn't a cute metaphor about chicken soup, oceans, or cheese either. Quite the contrary, it's meat and potatoes you can sink your teeth into.

If you were looking for a business book filled with graphs and stats, I apologize. But before you get disappointed, I would encourage you to suspend all judgment and let yourself be in for a surprise, a pleasant surprise. You are about to read and learn the battle-tested strategies used by the best in the business.

As you'll read in the coming pages, I'm not one to play it safe or stick to the middle of the road. The only things you find in the middle of the road are dotted lines and road kill. To get results no one else has gotten, you've got to get away from the middle of the road and head out to the edges of your industry. That's where the gold is. Traveling down the middle of the road is playing not to lose, it's playing it safe; that path is heavily trafficked, and you'll be among the mediocre many. If that's what you wanted, you wouldn't have picked up a book with the subtitle *Taking Your Business to the Big Time*.

Play to win and head out to the edge with me. Stadium status is about testing the limits and blazing your own trail in your industry. That's hard to do because you've got to have confidence, talent, courage, and perseverance, the exact same qualities you'll see in elite athletes and entertainers. Crazy? Maybe. Or maybe the rest of your industry competitors just aren't crazy enough.

Everybody thought Herb Kelleher was crazy when he launched Southwest Airlines and announced that his airline would get its planes up and down much faster than its competitors. The average turnaround time in the airline industry was an hour and a half—"turnaround" is the industry's term for the amount of time it takes to get a plane ready to take off again with a new set of passengers after deplaning the existing passengers upon arrival at the designated gate.

Southwest became famous for its twenty-minute turnaround. Kelleher got that crazy stadium status idea from watching pit crews at a NASCAR race, and to this day his employees use the pit crew model to handle deplaning a flight, prepping the plane, and reboarding the next set of passengers. Unlike its competition, Southwest treats the whole process of readying a plane for its next flight like a pit stop. Next time you fly Southwest, sit in the back of the plane so you're guaranteed to be the last person to exit when the plane lands—you'll see what I mean. Don't be surprised if you see the pilot pitching in to clean or pick up trash, too.

There was nothing middle of the road about Kelleher's strategy. He didn't play it safe and do what every one of his competitors was doing. He went to the edge and did things differently, and the stadium status idea that took Southwest to the big time was one he got from a completely different industry. That industry—stock car racing—coincidentally, began as the furthest thing from an actual sport. It began during prohibition when moonshine runners started souping up their cars so they could outrun federal agents as they transported liquor across state lines. The runs led to informal contests in which bootleggers raced one another to see who could run the fastest times. In 1947, these contests became organized as a sport under the National Association for Stock Car Auto Racing (NASCAR). The first NASCAR race was run in 1948 and the sport has since become America's biggest spectator sport.

That's right, the biggest stadium status sport in the United States got its start from another industry. Simply put, people who perform at the highest level and enjoy what they do got there by doing things differently. That's precisely what this book is all about: your best ideas will come from outside your industry and you, too, need to do things differently in order to reach Stadium Status in your field.

What This Book Is

The book you have in your hands represents an intersection of sports, entertainment, and business because I believe stadiums best epitomize the dreams we all have. While you may not aspire to appear before thousands in an actual stadium, I'm confident that rising to the top of your profession and attracting stadium-sized audiences for your work is your dream.

And what happens in the stadium doesn't have to stay in the stadium. This book will help you take the magic that happens under bright lights before thousands and translate it to your work and the brand that is uniquely you. The innovation, teamwork, and selflessness that embody the stadium status performer on stage and on the field will be revealed to you.

Athletes and entertainers see the world a little differently. They don't see black or white, rich or poor: they see teammates, teammates who sacrifice their egos to become a part of something bigger than themselves and reach a common goal every day. They persevere in the face of adversity and don't give up. Their stories inspire us. It's the reason that fans of music and sports, whether they are male or female, rich or poor, black or white, Republican or Democrat, fill stadium seats and cheer for their favorite artists and teams. Country music and sports unite and connect us in a way that nothing else does.

My entire life, stadiums have been my office, my sanctuary, and my happy place. Sometimes the world doesn't make a whole lot of sense to me, but what goes on in the stadium sure does. It's the prism through which I view the world and it is my inspiration for writing this book.

If there's one thing I've learned in my career as a coach and media personality, it's that both the sports and the music industries offer us the best model for solving many of our business problems. Is either industry without its problems? No, but a lifetime of experience in these arenas has shown me that the leadership principles and audience engagement strategies found in the stadium are far more effective than those you see in the typical workplace. You'd be hard-pressed to argue that championship-caliber teams and headlining musicians on Music Row in Nashville don't have more raving fans than almost anyone else you'll find in the business world. Who do you think is more popular, Garth Brooks or Alan Greenspan? The Dallas Cowboys or the IRS?

In sports and music, you see a level of audience engagement, teamwork, authenticity, and high performance that is freakishly uncommon outside the stadium. Why is it so uncommon? Because the worldview that athletes and entertainers possess is unique: both the sports and music industries teach competitors to look inward for resources and solutions. I was average, at best, as a collegiate athlete and as a college coach of underdog programs that had to do more with less. Yet, I thank God every day for these experiences because they provided invaluable life lessons that I apply to my approach as an executive coach and to my outlook as an entrepreneur.

This book will awaken you to the power of the strategies used by those who call the stadium their office, and it will help you elevate your business to stadium status in your own industry, whatever that may be. I will share these strategies with you through my own experience and through the experiences of musicians and leaders I respect for building a stadium status brand. The most powerful leadership strategy is leadership by example. With that in mind, I can't simply talk about stadium status without walking my talk. Otherwise, the book would be all theory and no practice, and you wouldn't know if any of it really worked.

The Stadium Map

Here's how you know these strategies are battle tested: at the beginning of all but chapter 1 (which sets the scene), I tell a stadium status story from performers or organizations that have taken their game to the big time. Then I share an anecdote that shows how I've applied the same strategy myself in my career as an entrepreneur and a college coach. Sometimes the story is about how my clients have applied the strategy to fit the "stadium" they work in, while other times it's about something that happened to me that illustrates the point. These stories are my way of showing you how these concepts work out in the marketplace.

Finally, we turn the focus to you and your business, so you can harness the power of the strategies in your own industry. The "Them," "Bru," and "You" format is your ticket to a deep dive into the application of a concept and how you can tailor it to your business. Clever, huh? To help you adapt the strategies to your own company, I've included a section called "Stadium Steps," which is a little coaching session at the end of each chapter. These coaching points help you map out a clear, actionable strategy that will let you apply the wisdom you gained and advance to stadium status in your industry. Ultimately, this book isn't just about what you can learn, it's about what you can execute. So if you don't answer the questions in the Stadium Steps as you go, you'll struggle to apply the wisdom all at once later. Do yourself a favor: answer the questions and take notes as you read—you'll thank me later.

How do you achieve stadium status? The same way you get a job with Gentle Giant Moving Company, by completing the stadium steps, literally. The Boston-based moving company requires that prospective employees be able to run all thirty-seven sections of Harvard Stadium's steps inside forty minutes. The company wants only the best movers so, to separate itself from the competition, Gentle Giant Moving seeks only employees who will perform at a high level.

Stadium status entrepreneurs do the same thing Gentle Giant CEO Larry O'Toole insists his team do: they go above and beyond. After unloading a box, Gentle Giant employees run back to the truck to pick up the next box. This sends a clear message to customers—and the competition—that these are true professionals who enjoy pushing themselves to perform at their highest level. As you will see, all stadium status performers go above and beyond.

Have you ever run stadium steps? Not the metaphorical ones I give you in this book, I mean *actual* stadium steps. It's the best workout you can imagine: challenging yet rewarding, intense yet motivating. This is my same goal for the stadium steps I share in each chapter. The stadium steps I assign as exercise will push you, they will challenge you to go above and beyond in order to perform at your highest level.

How do you do it? One step at a time. You've got this, now let's begin.

PART I

Vision

CHAPTER 1

#StadiumStatus

"Stadium status" is a term popularized by musicians and athletes. It's that elusive position every coach, athlete, entertainer, and performer strives to reach. It means moving from opening act to headliner, from a small stage to the greatest stage in the largest venue possible, a sold-out stadium. It's the same elusive position every entrepreneur strives to reach; it means moving from an also-ran to the biggest and best in class, from small accounts and a small customer base to a stadium full of raving fans.

Stadium status is a concept I learned from country music star Granger Smith and his manager Tyler Smith. Several years ago, they set their sights on achieving stadium status, and to keep their vision constantly in front of them, any time they had a new idea, reached a milestone, or grew their brand to the next level, they'd say the words "stadium status" to one another; they also took to signing their texts and e-mails to each other with #StadiumStatus.

Why is keeping your vision in front of you integral to winning? To understand how to win, we must first understand losing. It all starts in our minds. We create success—or failure—in our heads before we create it in the marketplace.

It Has to Be a Mentality before It's a Reality

Game Six of the 1986 World Series: the Boston Red Sox enjoyed a 5–3 lead in extra innings and were just three outs away from winning their first championship in 68 years. The New York Mets managed to tie the game, then they hit three straight singles, and on the very next at bat, Mookie Wilson hit a grounder that went up the first base line and through Bill Buckner's legs, allowing the winning run to score.

An ESPN E:60 documentary that aired on December 6, 2014, revealed that, just sixteen days before Game Six, Buckner was interviewed by Don Shane of WBZ-TV, and he described the pressures of postseason play, saying: "The dreams are that you're gonna have a great series and win. The nightmares are that you're gonna let the winning run score on a ground ball through your legs. Those things happen, you know. I think a lot of it is just fate."

What is now widely acknowledged as one of the costliest errors in sports history may never have happened if Buckner had protected his confidence and maintained a better vision of his future. What happened to Bill Buckner can and does happen to all of us on a different scale every day.

Contrast Buckner's thoughts with Babe Ruth's fifty-four years earlier. When Ruth came to bat in the fifth inning of Game 3 of the 1932 World Series, Cubs fans and players were heckling and taunting him. To get in their heads, or perhaps to get them out of his, Ruth pointed his bat over the center field fence. One pitch later, the Sultan of Swat hit his second home run of the game, and the Yankees went on to a 7–5 win.

I realize you may not be a baseball fan and may not have even been alive for either event, so think about how having a strong vision works in the context of your job. When we're under pressure, we talk ourselves into and out of things. For example, our minds don't have the ability to correctly process the word "don't." In other words, focusing on *not* doing something often causes us to do that very thing. Have you ever played golf and stepped up to the ball while thinking to yourself, "Don't hit it in the bunker" or "Don't slice the ball," only to go on and hit it in the bunker or slice it? Like Ruth, we are better served when we focus on what we want, not what we don't want.

A year after Buckner's error, psychologist Daniel Wegner performed a research study that explored the way people suppressed their thoughts. Participants were asked to articulate their thoughts nonstop for five minutes and to ring a bell if they thought of or verbalized a white bear. Wegner gave very specific instructions just before the start of the five-minute period. He told them, "Try not to think of a white bear."

What happened next was essentially Buckner's error all over again. The participants became fixated on the white bear. This experiment revealed that when you're told not to think about something, you begin effectively subliminally advertising that very thing to yourself.

How to Protect Your Belief System

To help avoid unwanted thoughts, use affirmations, like Granger Smith's band uses #StadiumStatus. Repeating what you *do* want (not what you want to avoid) will enhance your belief, and when you enhance your belief you will enhance your results. If you think something often enough, it becomes a part of you.

When I interviewed Granger Smith and his drummer, Dusty Saxton, Saxton shared with me a critical juncture in the band's journey. A number of years ago, after a show that was less than stellar, Saxton told the band, "Listen, guys, I'll be playing stadiums one day, whether it's with this band or another band."

He was reaffirming his vision and, in the process, refocusing his bandmates. I believe, like Saxton, that you have a responsibility to have a bigger vision for the people around you than they sometimes have for themselves. As a result of Saxton's words, the band now uses the stadium status mantra not just on good days but also when things go wrong, in order to reinforce their vision to themselves. Band members embrace and repeat this mantra consistently, and Smith attributes this as a key to their success: "For a band member who might be doubtful a couple years ago, hearing everyone repeat this is reinforcement of their collective vision."

The band has gone from playing small markets to stadium status, and was recently announced as an "On the Verge" artist by iHeart radio. Make no mistake about it, Smith is an entrepreneur, and the lesson for the entrepreneur in Smith's rise to stadium status lies in the words he shared with me: "It's not about talent or work ethic. That's just enough to get you in the door because a lot of people have talent and work ethic. It's about strategy, too. My talent was good enough to get me in the game; after that, it's up to me how I play the game."

Whether you're an entrepreneur, a baseball player, or a musician, you're either growing or dying; there's no standing still. Talent and work ethic might get you in the game, but stadium status takes strategy. Your strategy, like Smith's, must start with a vision.

Nobody starts out at stadium status. Every artist or player starts from humble beginnings. Smith's stadium status journey began with his first album in 1998; eighteen years later Smith and his band, by steadily maintaining and reinforcing their vision, have built a stadium status brand. Granger Smith's story is a testament to the fact that what many may view as an overnight success is actually thousands of nights in the making.

Your journey can be intimidating, frustrating, painful, and sometimes downright humbling. What makes it a lot easier is having great teammates. Great teammates help you get your mind set for success and protect your confidence every step of the way toward stadium status.

You need to spend time with people who not only share your vision but have a vision that is bigger than yours. Keeping that kind of company forces you to step your game up. Who supports your bigger vision?

The only way you can keep moving forward with positive momentum is to protect your confidence every day. One of the best ways to protect your confidence is to be very selective in the people you surround yourself with. Who do you spend most of your time with? Who is in your peer group? Do the people around you support you and lift you up?

Psychologist Dr. Milton Erickson is famous for writing in a patient's chart, then excusing himself and stepping out of the office for a couple of minutes. When the patient would peek at the chart, he or she would see, "Doing well" written there. If that isn't the best kind of therapy, I don't know what is.

As you've learned from stadium status performers like Babe Ruth and Granger Smith, and from psychologists Daniel Wegner and Milton Erickson, regardless of what "it" is, it has to be a mentality before it's a reality. Consider the context in which you should be using #StadiumStatus as a message, an advertisement, and a reminder to your team that reinforces your collective vision. I cannot emphasize the importance of this enough because, as you'll see demonstrated in the next chapter, a leader's vision is contagious and sets the trajectory for the team's performance.

CHAPTER 2

Be the First Believer

Lose and go home, survive and advance.

—Jim Valvano, basketball coach

In college basketball, 351 teams start the season, four play in the championship stadium, and only one wins it all. All things being equal (which they aren't), that's a 0.002 percent chance of winning the championship. So, for an underdog, the odds are actually even worse. How do the four teams arrive at the stadium, and how will the champion be crowned? Many would say the important things happened on the court in previous rounds. Others would say the teams earned their way into the championship tournament during conference tournaments. I'm here to tell you that the teams' victories happened way before that, because championships are scheduled. I'm referring here to the power of intentionality. You need to have a process in place to cast your vision and achieve your goals, because success doesn't happen by accident.

You can influence what you want to happen by practicing intentionality. Your success also happens way before it actually manifests itself. If your goal is to win a championship in your industry or to perform on the biggest stage, you need to see yourself there in your mind before the goal can manifest; you must arrive at the place mentally before you can arrive at the physical destination and compete in the championship stadium.

Them

Legendary North Carolina State basketball coach Jim Valvano devoted the first day of practice every season to something very unorthodox, maybe even downright weird by many standards. For the first practice there were no basketballs, no drills, and no scrimmages, just a ladder, a pair of scissors, and a vision. Valvano would have his players practice cutting down the nets, to simulate what they would do when they won the national championship. Not if—when. What is the benefit of practicing this? Valvano wanted his players to paint a picture in their minds of themselves as winners and to believe in themselves even if no one else did. It's not enough to tell your team to "visualize" winning; you've got to actually commit to practicing it in a hands-on way to make it real. The North Carolina team even filmed their practice net-cutting, and would watch the replay in the locker room throughout the season.

Six months after their first practice, Valvano's 1983 Wolfpack team turned this preseason vision into reality when they won the NCAA Championship. They had ten losses on the season and were fifty to one underdogs, but aren't we all?

The coach's belief in his team was reinforced by his family, specifically his father. When Valvano became a college head coach, he told his dad he was going to win a national championship. While he was visiting his parents, Valvano's dad called him up to the bedroom and showed him a suitcase. He explained to his son that his bag was packed; he was ready for the day his son would win the national championship. He would be there. His bag was already packed. This is perhaps the greatest gift we can give people we lead: the gift of belief.

When anyone achieves great success, you can rest assured that he had to overcome great adversity. Our trials make our triumphs that much sweeter. You might be really far away from your goal, and sharing your vision might lead the people around you to think you're delusional, but that shared vision also gives them a vivid memory to carry with them and focus their mind on during the trials. Sometimes it's just a game, and sometimes those trials are life or death.

I was reminded of how our trials can become our triumphs in an interview with the band Parmalee. Parmalee consists of brothers Matt and Scott Thomas, their cousin Barry Knox, and lifelong friend Josh McSwain. The four grew up about an hour down Route 64 from NC State's campus, in Parmele, North Carolina, population 276. What are the odds of a family band making it from Parmele to the heights of fame in Nashville? To quote Parmalee bassist Barry Knox, probably less than 5 percent. Five percent is also the odds of survival given Parmalee's drummer, Scott Thomas, in September of 2010.

In September 2010, the members of Parmalee were involved in an attempted robbery and a shootout in their RV outside a club they had just played. The incident came on the eve of a showcase with Stoney Creek Records, the reason the band was traveling to Nashville. Scott Thomas was shot three times and was airlifted to a hospital in Charlotte. He was given a 5 percent chance of living by doctors, but miraculously pulled through after spending thirty-five days in the hospital, ten of them in a coma.

When I asked the band about the ordeal, they all framed their reaction as focusing on the 5 percent chance of survival, not the 95 percent chance of death. Why? Because they maintained a belief and a vision that enabled them to always bet on themselves, in spite of evidence that the situation was dire.

At one point, the band's credit card debt was over $100,000. Matt Thomas commented that the interest rate on his debt was at a whopping 36 percent.

Still, Parmalee didn't take no for an answer; they maintained their belief and kept working. Scott Thomas did indeed recover. The band made it to Nashville, landed a contract with Stoney Creek, and now has a number-one song and two top-ten songs to their credit. Parmalee didn't survive and advance because they're simply overachievers; they've won because they're first and foremost overbelievers. "I think we've always looked at it from the stadium backward," Matt Thomas said. "We always thought big, and it's really cool to be able to get onstage now and see the amount of people, and be able to have that energy."

Are you looking at your business from the stadium backward? Are you dreaming big and believing even bigger, in spite of current evidence?

Bru

I can relate to Valvano and Parmalee because I, too, have always looked at things from the stadium backward. Valvano wanted to make sure his players believed they would win the national championship, expected to win it, and prepared for exactly how they would respond when it happened. During my years as a college lacrosse coach (just miles down the road from both Raleigh and Parmele), Valvano's story stuck with me and led me to write the National Championship game into our team's schedule each year. Seeing that on the calendar gave our players confidence, and I consistently got feedback from recruits that seeing that vision made them attracted to us.

For more than a few years, we would begin the season with what I like to call the National Championship drill. With our starters on the field and the remaining players on the sidelines, we'd turn the scoreboard on with us in the lead and ten seconds left on the clock. When the clock hit zero and the horn sounded, our players would rush the field and dogpile on their teammates in celebration. I wanted the players to set their sights and their intentions on that outcome. I wanted them to make it as real as possible—to see it, touch it, feel it, and experience it before it happened. I also wanted them to know how to respond when it happened. After all, like everything else, championships are scheduled.

Hindsight being what it is, I should add this disclaimer. Rushing the field, cutting the nets down, and similar exercises don't work every year. Case in point: in 2003, after losing in the NCAA Final Four the year before, I wanted to paint a picture of our end goal in my players' minds. So, during our individual preseason meetings, I had each player get sized for a championship ring. I wanted them to think big, visualize the ring as it would appear on their fingers, and cement that memory in their minds. Fast-forward a few months; we were mediocre at best, and had one of our worst seasons on record. You can't win 'em all.

Whatever your goal, look from the stadium backward. Just as I took our schedule and worked backward from the National Championship game each year, you can do the same with your vision. For example, when my client

Nathan Wadsworth first ran for political office at the beginning of his campaign, we didn't just circle Election Day on the calendar and then make a campaign game plan "hoping to win." We made sure everyone knew he expected to win, so we also scheduled the victory party, right down to the time and location. From that minute forward, the intention and the vision were set for Nate and his team. Remember, championships are scheduled in all sorts of arenas.

You

Valvano's team had less than a 2 percent chance of winning; Scott Thomas had a 5 percent chance of surviving his injuries. The odds of success are stacked against all of us, and we have to be the first believers when it comes to our business. Your belief may not run the world, but it sure does run your world. Are you going all in and betting on yourself? You need to, because your belief is contagious. And when others believe in you it becomes harder for any doubts to creep in. Your people need you to believe in them and to set high expectations.

Perhaps your vision is for a new location, multiple offices, a bigger footprint of the area your business services, or perhaps it involves preparing an acceptance speech for an award you've set your sights on, or maybe it's simply a numeric goal like ten times growth. Whatever your goal, it all begins with a vision, and in order to accomplish anything of significance you have to be your own first believer. Dream the dream and believe you can achieve it.

Stadium Steps

1. How are you looking at your business from the stadium backward? You've got to be able to visualize the end goal. Turn your imagination loose and describe what that goal looks like in detail.
2. Like Parmalee, can you maintain belief in spite of the current evidence? Your belief may not run the world, but it sure does run your world.
3. Do you have a vision for victory and have you practiced cutting down the nets?
4. The greatest gift you can give people is belief in them. Who do you need to demonstrate your belief to? How will you do it? Schedule it.

CHAPTER 3

Your Golden Ticket

There's one in every crowd and it's usually me.
—Montgomery Gentry, American country music duo

The pass reads ALL ACCESS in big, bold, capital letters. Whether fans receive these laminated passes by winning a contest on the radio, being a fan club member, or simply paying for them, a lucky few will get premium access to their favorite artists or players. At a concert, an all-access pass punches your ticket to go backstage in the green room and meet the artist, get pictures taken together, and, in some instances even appear on stage or hop aboard the tour bus. At sporting events, your all-access pass will get you a tour of the locker room, where you can listen to the pregame talk, and access to the sidelines during games.

Consumers are willing to purchase access to just about everywhere worth going, and they look to avoid the crowds while doing it. And the only thing better than purchasing access is winning it for free—as you do with a golden ticket. It's kind of like the way a meal always tastes better when someone else is buying.

The idea of the golden ticket dates back to Roald Dahl's 1964 book *Charlie and the Chocolate Factory*. The character Willy Wonka decided to open his factory to five kids and their parents for a behind-the-scenes tour and a lifetime supply of Wonka candy. In order to determine which kids would win a chance to visit the factory, Wonka hid five golden tickets inside the wrappers of his chocolate bars. Wonka's goal was to significantly raise chocolate bar sales; he accomplished that mission, and then some. If you've read the book you'll recall parents buying up chocolate bars by the dozen. To ensure his daughter would be a winner, Veruca Salt's dad bought a truckload of bars, while the other kids emptied out their piggy banks to get a chance to win one of the coveted tickets.

Wonka's stunt created media hype and a buzz among consumers. The public became fascinated with who would win the five tickets. The concept of a golden ticket can create a sense of excitement and cement brand loyalty unlike anything else. It's unique, it's a gift, and it's a surprise. Everyone loves winning a surprise.

Let me overcome the objection you're already thinking about. "How much is this going to cost me? Custom motorcycles, a vacation at a resort, or a cruise? Those sound expensive." Yes, there's going to be a cost associated with creating this kind of campaign, but don't think of it as an expense. We are talking about an investment. People don't need more ways to buy your product or service, they need more reasons to buy. When you create a golden ticket you create goodwill, which is a good reason. Too many businesses think purely in terms of costs and ROI (return on investment). What we are doing here is deeper than that. What we're talking about is *ROR,* return on relationship. You're adding enormous value and, as a result, creating enormous goodwill, which in turn strengthens, deepens, and expands your relationships. There is an absolute return on relationship when it comes to offering a golden ticket. You get people even more excited about something they already love—your brand.

Them

On October 18, 2011, Eddie Montgomery and Troy Gentry of the duo Montgomery Gentry borrowed a page from Willy Wonka's playbook when they released their album *Rebels on the Run.* For three weeks leading up to the release date, fans could become eligible to win the golden ticket by preordering the album on the band's website. One lucky fan who preordered the album would be surprised with a golden ticket inside the CD case. That ticket won the fan a custom motorcycle from Demented Cycles, which partnered with the duo on the golden ticket promotion. The promotion created a huge media buzz, indirectly selling the new album and generating a fascinating human interest story, because Montgomery and Gentry both had a hand in designing the one-of-a-kind bike. This was the first-ever golden ticket associated with an album release and, like Wonka's lifetime supply of candy, it was an extravagant, expensive surprise.

The golden ticket that University of Nebraska football coach Mike Riley deploys is a little more subtle. Per NCAA rules, at midnight on August 1, colleges can extend scholarship offers to high school seniors, and at that time Coach Riley channels his inner Willy Wonka. While most college teams simply send out an offer on letterhead or perhaps dispatch a colorful one-sheeter with the offer printed on it, Coach Riley is "the one" in every crowd. Nebraska sends its recruits a golden ticket that reveals the $190,000 total value of the scholarship offer and highlights all the perks associated with it:

- MacBook Air laptop
- iPad
- 3,300 dining hall meals
- $4,400 in weekend meals at downtown restaurants
- $20,000 in athletic apparel
- $7,500 in post-eligibility scholarship money students can utilize to finish their degree.

Most of Nebraska's competition doesn't highlight the features and benefits specific to their scholarship offers, nor do they lead the offer letter with the impressive financial commitment they are making to their students. They simply say, "Congratulations" or, "We want you at XYZ University." If you're a top prospect, you're receiving a hundred or more scholarship offers on August 1. Which one do you think stands out in the crowd—tired, boring old letterhead or a golden ticket?

Bru

I don't just preach, I practice the strategies I'm sharing. One lucky reader who preordered this book was surprised with my version of Montgomery Gentry's golden ticket. That golden ticket won the reader a three-day, two-night stay for two at the Henderson Beach Resort in Destin, Florida, complete with a toes-in-the-sand dinner. For the month leading up to the release date of *Stadium Status*, my fans could become eligible to win the golden ticket by preordering the book on my website, www.stadiumstatusbook.com. Additionally, there were silver and bronze tickets given away during the book launch, thanks to the generosity of my sponsors and strategic partners. Perhaps you won one of them? We partnered with Lawrence Hunt fashions to give away a dozen men's and women's performance dress shirts to silver ticket winners. Two dozen bronze ticket winners received Stadium Status T-shirts from 207 Ink wearable art. To surprise and delight still others, we randomly selected folks who preordered *Stadium Status* and sent them care packages containing my other books as well.

Although you may not have won a golden ticket, there is still plenty of value in heading over to the website. You can sign up to receive a link to a playlist featuring music from the artists featured in the pages of this book, along with other surprise bonuses and resources. It's my gift to you and my way of saying thank you for investing in and sharing the message of this book.

I've been using the concept of the golden ticket since 2004. That was the year I retired from college coaching and worked as a talk show host and sales manager of a group of ESPN Radio affiliates in the Carolinas. To create buzz about the stations and my show, and to add value for our advertisers, I created a golden ticket promotion. We partnered with the Carolina Panthers NFL franchise and a local travel agent to provide a pair of lucky winners with an all-expenses-paid cruise to the Caribbean with several Panthers players. In order to enter the contest, listeners had to show up at our participating advertisers' stores to sign up for the drawing. At the end of the month-long promotion, one lucky winner took home the golden ticket.

This golden ticket promotion was a win-win on many fronts. First and foremost, it increased our audience engagement, not only with the station but with our advertisers, because the promotion drove our listeners to their doorsteps, literally. Selling radio advertising is selling the invisible (air), and without direct action by listeners, it's hard to quantify your return on investment. With

Figure 3.1 *Golden ticket*

the golden ticket, we took something intangible and qualitative and made it tangible and quantitative for our clients by creating a one-to-one relationship on their home turf, between them and our audience. Furthermore, the promotion cemented our relationship with both listeners and advertisers. Our listeners were excited we were doing something different, something no other station had done before, and that they had an opportunity to participate. Several who didn't win the golden ticket were so excited about the opportunity to go on the cruise that they purchased tickets from our advertising partner's travel agency. And all of the sign-up locations were thrilled that we drove customers to their doors, because many of the listeners who came to sign up at their places of business also spent money shopping there. It was a win-win-win all the way around.

You

A custom motorcycle or a cruise may not be your thing but, figuratively speaking, we all are sitting on a golden ticket with our businesses. A golden ticket can be any unique opportunity in the form of a synergistic relationship, sponsorship, or marketing partnership that differentiates you and your strategic partners from the rest of the competition in a crowded marketplace. We just need to identify that golden opportunity and share it with the world in a creative way. In the literal sense, a golden ticket promotion like Montgomery Gentry's provides you with a great way to surprise and delight your fans and add some buzz leading up to a landmark day in the life of your business. Perhaps it's a grand opening of a new location, the launch of a new product or service, or the celebration of a holiday sale—whatever the event, you can execute a golden ticket strategy. Maybe your customer demographic wouldn't be interested in a custom chopper from Demented Cycles but, like I did, you can tailor your prizes to fit your audience.

You don't have to be an artist, athlete, or author to create golden tickets or backstage passes. In every industry there are fans who want an exclusive sneak peek behind the scenes to see what you've got going on. When you bring them behind the scenes or on board your bus and let them see who you are, what you're about, and how the "secret sauce" of your operation gets made, they will be forever grateful. Every Friday afternoon, Bourgeois Guitar, a custom guitar maker in Lewiston, Maine, opens its doors to the public and school groups for tours of the facility. People love it.

These kinds of behind-the-scenes looks let your fans see your business from the other side; they get a glimpse at your perspective and can see the world through your eyes. Perhaps even more valuable is the fact that the fans' access does a similar thing for you. You become closer to your customers, perhaps even friends. You get to have fun with them in a way that is different, outside the normal business-to-consumer relationship, which is often just transactional.

Harness the Power of Strategic Partners

When I worked in radio, I made a point having our station serve as the conduit between a number of local businesses, both via our golden ticket promotion and by connecting business owners who had complementary or synergistic services. Now I help my coaching clients do the same in their markets. You can take a page out of that playbook by trading services with other, synergistic businesses to offer prizes and special events to your customers. The beauty of finding synergistic businesses is that there is no competing interest; you are each highly referable to the other and motivated to help. Everybody wins.

Think of the enormous potential for each and every one of the following businesses, which all serve the same clientele in their own unique way: florist, wedding dress shop, caterer, banquet hall, tuxedo shop, photographer, videographer, and disc jockey/emcee. Each could offer customers a unique golden ticket based on prizes from another of the businesses.

Travel Agency	Grand Prize—Trip for two to an exotic destination
Hotel	Weekend stay for two
Airline	Two tickets to the destination
Restaurant	Romantic dinner for two
Florist	Flowers
Chocolatier	Custom candy boxes
Photographer	One free sitting

Premium Pays

People will pay a premium for access and convenience. In the eastern United States, much of the interstate system offers E-ZPass, an electronic toll collection express lane that allows you to avoid waiting in line to pay tolls on bridges and highways from Maine to North Carolina. Disney offers FastPass service, which, for a premium fee, gets you bumped to the front of lines at Disney theme parks. And almost every commercial airline offers priority boarding. The Department of Homeland Security offers TSA Pre and Global Entry, which is a service that, for an $85 fee (assuming you pass the online background check and in-person interview), allows you to receive a prechecked security screening at the airport. It's essentially Disney's FastPass for air travel. You pay for the convenience of bypassing the security line, and you don't need to remove your shoes or take your laptop out of your briefcase when you pass through the air-port security checkpoint. It was the best $85 I've ever spent in my life. In each of these cases, customers happily pay a premium to receive either faster access or greater access, together with a significantly more convenient experience.

You will stay stuck in traffic fighting to inch your way ahead until you look at your business differently and realize there is a population of your clients and prospects who are willing to pay a premium for convenience. I share this with you because not everyone wants to leave the golden ticket up to chance and, like Veruca Salt's dad in *Charlie and the Chocolate Factory*, some are willing to pay a premium to guarantee access. Many entertainers offer a VIP experience at their concerts, giving fans the chance to pay a premium to attend a private meet-and-greet in the green room and even on the tour bus. My premium offer is my platinum-level coaching program. I offer a limited number of clients an opportunity to participate in this program, and it includes priority scheduling and unlimited access to me 24–7 via phone and e-mail, as well as complimen-tary tickets to the public programs and workshops I offer throughout the year.

You don't need to reinvent the wheel to create a premium offer in your business. You can do so by taking your current product and service offerings, adding value, and supercharging them by bundling or packaging them with additional bonuses. Perhaps your brand might benefit from an app that pro-vides users with early bird or exclusive access to sales, events, and promotions. The bonus is for you to decide, but providing value at a premium will, without a doubt, move you into the express lane, fast-tracking your business growth.

Stadium Steps

1. Have your team brainstorm golden ticket opportunities (new product launch, grand opening, anniversary celebration, etc.).
2. Create a list of your ideal strategic partners and then approach them with your ideas. Make the promotion a win-win for them.
3. Remember: K − A = 0, or, knowledge minus action equals zero. So, execute the promotion. Make a note of the event or product and the date by which you are committing to execute your Golden Ticket.
4. Think about the premium services you can and should offer your best clients. Wait . . . Before you answer that, ask them. Your clients will tell you everything you need to know to serve them better.

CHAPTER 4

A Rising Tide

A rising tide raises all ships.
—Slogan of the New England Regional Chamber of Commerce

I love Nashville. What I love about Music City, specifically, is the musician mindset. Every night there are three hundred to four hundred musicians performing live, for free, with the hope of getting discovered. The most fascinating thing is that they all want to see each other succeed. This is a foreign concept to a lot of businesspeople and definitely to a lot of coaches. These people are focused on competition instead of creation.

This was definitely the case with Bill, a former coaching colleague of mine. An opposing team in his conference was playing in the National Championship game, and I was surprised when Bill told me he wasn't rooting for them. (Note: no team in his conference had ever won a national championship.) I was disappointed to hear his attitude because he didn't realize that his competitor winning would have actually helped him and his program in the long run.

Sometimes the student is the teacher. My first year as a college head coach, I was recruiting a blue-chip athlete named Stephen who had just about every college, big and small, knocking down his door. We weren't very good at the time and I had been hired so late in the summer that I was behind in the recruiting process, so you can imagine my surprise when we turned out to be Stephen's top choice.

When I asked him to formally commit and sign his national letter of intent during the early signing period in the fall, he refused, indicating that he wanted to wait but was willing to give a nonbinding verbal commitment. I was desperate for talent and, knowing he was way better than anyone else we were recruiting, I told him I would hold a scholarship for him until he was ready to commit in the spring, no pressure.

Fall turned to winter and other coaches kept coming to Stephen's games and recruiting him hard; winter turned to spring and the cycle repeated itself. When his high school coach and I pressed him to commit, Stephen said something that left me thunderstruck:

> Coach, I don't know if you've noticed, but a lot of colleges come to see me play each week. Most of my teammates weren't getting scholarship offers or even being recruited earlier this year but now they are. By me not committing anywhere, all the college coaches who keep coming to see me play get a chance to discover how good some of my teammates really are. If I signed early with you, all the other coaches would've stopped coming to the games and none of my teammates would've gotten recruited.

By delaying signing with a college, this student athlete revealed a wisdom and maturity well beyond his seventeen years. I never in a million years thought I would've allowed a prospect to dictate deadlines in the recruiting process, especially after the signing date came and went, but at that point I understood he was the ultimate team player. So I agreed to let him wait until the end of the season to sign with us. Stephen was a man of his word, and signed with us at the end of the season; and, as a result of his delay, many of his teammates got college scholarships. The original reason every recruiter wanted him was for his talent on the field; little did I know that Stephen would reveal to me through his character an even bigger, better reason that he was worth waiting for.

There's an old saying "A rising tide raises all ships." That concept isn't limited to boats in the harbor, it applies to the work we each do. It's about embracing an abundance mindset rather than having a scarcity mentality.

Iron sharpens iron, and winners help other people win. The musicians in Nashville all want to see one another succeed because they know that when country music as a whole is stronger, each of them is stronger. Look no further than artists on "competing" record labels touring together and promoting one another's new albums upon release.

Them

The example that best reveals this team-focused mindset is Brian Kelley and Tyler Hubbard, of the duo Florida-Georgia Line, cowriting "Burnin' It Down" with Chris Tompkins and Rodney Clawson. The four artists originally wrote the song with the intention that they'd record it themselves. Instead, they decided that Jason Aldean's voice and musical style would be perfectly suited for the song.

Perfect is an understatement. "Burnin' It Down" went on to become Aldean's twelfth number-one single, earned platinum status (more than one million units sold), and turned out to be his fastest-breaking single to date. Could Florida-Georgia Line have kept the song for themselves and saved it for their next album? Sure, but as songwriters they embrace the creator's mindset and know that the best thing for their industry collectively is to perfectly match the song with the right artist. Aldean's "Burnin' It Down" tour epitomized stadium status, as he played many of America's football and baseball stadiums while on that tour. With more than two million tickets sold, Aldean played before massive crowds in some of the most iconic stadiums: Lambeau Field in Green Bay, Wisconsin; Gillette Stadium in Foxborough, Massachusetts; and the Rose Bowl in Pasadena, California. And he broke Pink Floyd's record in Kansas City's Arrowhead Stadium by performing before more than 57,000 fans.

The creator's mindset is what I love most about my career as an author and speaker. It's also what I love about country musicians. They know that creating more fans of their genre benefits the entire industry. They don't believe there are limited pieces of the pie and they have to angle to get their share. They aren't about competing—they're about creating. To them, the pie is unlimited. Their competition isn't the artist across the street on music row; instead, they view their competition as the person looking at them in the mirror each morning.

Bru

Years ago, one of my first consulting clients was a beer company; that company will remain nameless, but let's just say it didn't exactly produce the king of beers. The vice president informed me that company employees didn't drink other brands of beer; they'd be fired if they were ever caught drinking a competing brand. They're expected to be 100 percent loyal to the brand at all times. I quickly learned that the beverage industry is basically a turf war and that Budweiser, Coors, and Miller are the three biggest gangs in the neighborhood. These brands view the others as the enemy and are constantly competing to gain additional retail shelf space at the expense of the others. Essentially, they do their best to convince retailers to take some of the competition's real estate and give it to them. At times, sales reps even sabotage competitors' in-store displays and product placement. If they had it their way, I think they'd all give their right arms to have theirs be the only brand on the shelf and own the entire category in stores. It's a scarcity mindset.

This remains such a foreign concept to me. Authors don't compete; we create. Almost everyone in my profession has an abundance mindset. We actually like one another, and we read and promote one another's books. We share readily and believe that gaining more readers of more books is a good thing for all of us. It is the same with speaking. Professional speakers operate on the belief that good speaking begets good speaking. If you're performing exemplary work, it's not bad for me, it's good for the entire industry. We aren't trying to own the shelf space in the bookstore or run other speakers out of our profession. Instead, we want to share space with other winners. We spend our money to buy, read, and recommend other authors' books. Can you imagine the president of Budweiser recommending a Coors product to his colleagues?

While the major-label beer companies operate out of scarcity, there is a portion of the industry that embrace the creator's mindset: the micro and craft breweries. These smaller companies possess an entrepreneurial spirit, and realize that they rise and fall together. Their audience tends to be passionate rather than casual beer drinkers. They are people who appreciate the craftsmanship that goes into creating. In 2015 my hometown of Portland, Maine, was voted the top beer city in the United States. There are seventeen microbreweries in a city with a population under 100,000, and the city plays host to the New England Brew Summit. Many of these breweries neighbor one another on the same road, and it's not uncommon to see one lend ingredients to another if that neighbor runs out. They embrace the idea that true success means rooting for everyone. I find it no small coincidence that one of the breweries is aptly named Rising Tide Brewing Company.

The beer industry as a whole might be in better shape if everyone embraced the idea that more aficionados of beer, whether it's their beer or not, are good for everyone's business. Don't hold your breath waiting for that to happen with the big brands, though.

You

Do you root for your competition? If your answer is "no," let's reframe that to "not yet." The best thing you can do for yourself and your entire profession is to actually root for the competition, not to beat you but rather to strengthen your entire profession. As my colleague Dr. Rob Bell likes to say, "True success means rooting for everybody." When you root for everybody you approach your industry from an abundance mindset rather than one of scarcity. What you will find is that this abundance-based belief system is contagious.

This contagion works through a concept in social psychology called the law of reciprocity. The law of reciprocity is essentially a social rule that expects people to repay or give back in kind the treatment they receive from another person. This reciprocity rule relates directly to you and your industry peers because it engenders a sense of obligation to give back when someone performs a kind act or favor for you (even if that person is a competitor). When one party invests in a relationship with another by doing a kind act or favor, or by showing generosity, an imbalance naturally occurs in the dynamics of that relationship.

When you invest in relationships with competitors in your industry, you generate a sense of goodwill, respect, and trust among your peers. They then feel a natural desire to reciprocate and find ways or opportunities to help you as well. I'm sure you've heard the expression, "I'll scratch your back if you scratch mine" and "One hand washes the other"; while these may be clichés, there is an undeniable truth to the underlying message. After all, there's a reason that brands give free samples to customers at the grocery store; the recipient of the sample feels compelled to reciprocate by purchasing that brand instead of a different one. Keep in mind that in many industries the reciprocal act won't be as immediate as that of the consumer who just sampled a piece of cheddar cheese at the deli counter and decides to purchase that brand's product.

You don't have to give away product or your financial resources to help someone in your field. Perhaps your investment is sharing ideas or resources with others in your profession. It could also take the form of your time, mentorship, or even emotional support. All of these approaches are better than simply sharing product or throwing money at a relationship, because they demonstrate that your intent is to be sincere and thoughtful. Offering just cash or product involves less thought, and some may view that sort of gesture as manipulation rather than facilitation (casinos that give gamblers free drinks provide one example of manipulation rather than a sincere gesture). When you give your time and intellectual resources, you send a genuine message that your intentions are pure and you sincerely want to help others.

You are going to be viewed as a trustworthy and respected resource within the profession rather than simply a competitor. There's a big difference between the way we treat our adversaries versus our allies, isn't there? When you put the law of reciprocity into play, you will enjoy a positive cumulative effect that derives from helping others in your industry. And you will soon see that a rising tide does indeed raise all of your ships.

Stadium Steps

1. Just like Stephen, the student athlete, helped all his teammates, winners help other people win. Note three specific ways you can you help others in your profession get a win, and in the process collectively strengthen your industry.
2. Just as the beer industry is only as strong as the worst-tasting beer, you're only as strong as the worst competitor in your space. Commit to one thing you will do to help lift up another member of your professional community.
3. Who can you "tour with" in your industry to market and cross promote each other's work?

CHAPTER 5

Fearless Authenticity

Hard times arouse an instinctive desire for authenticity.

—Coco Chanel

Normally, entertainers arrive on the red carpet at awards shows in a limo. Granger Smith is not normal. He insisted on traveling to the 2015 Country Music Awards in a Chevy Silverado. It's authentically who he is. Smith has always owned a Silverado, and it's what his "customers" expect from him.

It reminded me of a similar incident twenty years earlier, at the Academy of Country Music awards, when Alan Jackson walked the red carpet in jeans and a T-shirt. During his performance on stage that night, he had his drummer play without drumsticks. The show producers told Jackson to "play along" with a prerecorded track. Jackson disagreed because it was inauthentic, so having his drummer play along without drumsticks was his weird way of clueing in his audience. He walked away with the Top Male Vocalist award that year, and, I would argue, his authenticity is precisely why fans love him.

Neither Smith nor Jackson was afraid to make a statement. How about you? We should all strive to be more like them, because we are all entertainers, delivering a performance every time we step on the stage that is our business. If your performance isn't authentic, it won't resonate.

Simply put, authenticity is staying true to who you are and what you do. You can't *act* authentic, you can only *be* authentic. Authenticity is built around substance and purpose. As cowboys like to say, don't be all hat and no cattle. In other words, don't make claims you can't back up.

Volkswagen's fudging of the numbers on its vehicles' emissions standards and claiming to be "the eco-friendly automotive manufacturer" serves as a great cautionary tale of the perils of being all hat and no cattle. The media referred to Volkswagen's dodge as the "diesel dupe" after the Environmental Protection Agency found that many Volkswagen vehicles sold in the United States came with factory-installed software in its diesel engines that cheated the system. The software could tell when emissions tests were being performed on the engines and it automatically fudged the engine's performance numbers so it would score better on the test. Volkswagen later admitted that more than eleven million cars sold contained this software, including Porsche and Audi models manufactured by Volkswagen. To say the least, the scandal showed that the car manufacturer was a far cry from an authentically eco-friendly company, and it had quite a damaging effect on Volkswagen's brand equity.

Them

Remember in late 2009, when Domino's launched a campaign admitting its pizza was lousy and introduced a completely new recipe with a money-back guarantee on its pizza? Its honesty and transparency resulted in revenue growth of 14.3 percent in the first quarter of 2010, and since then Domino's stock has risen 400 percent. Criticizing your own product is weird; it's also authentic and memorable. Why? Because it builds substance, and your authenticity turns customers into fanatics.

In the fall of 2015, I attended Brett Eldredge's Suits and Boots concert in Bangor, Maine, and got a glimpse into one of the finest demonstrations of authenticity in action you'll ever witness in any industry. Eldredge shared with the audience how nervous he was five years earlier, on his first major stadium tour, when he opened for Tim McGraw at the same venue. Eldredge told the sold-out arena that he'd always appreciated how receptive and forgiving the crowd was, even though he was so nervous he practically forgot the lyrics to his own song at one point. It was a dangerous but fearlessly authentic thing to admit, and it got him a standing ovation between songs. (Nobody gets a standing ovation between songs. During, yes, between, no.)

We in the audience witnessed a performance by someone who wasn't trying to impress us; instead, he told stories of his career and that embarrassing moment five years earlier. He was on a stage but not on a pedestal. There were no walls and no filter—it was about connection. The experience encouraged me to reflect on who I am and what I do. I encourage you to reflect on the authenticity you bring to your work and live out in your personal life as well.

No one understands and embraces this better than Jon Loba, executive vice president of BBR Music Group. Loba shared with me that what attracted BBR to the artists they've signed is their authenticity and uniqueness. Loba explained:

Many artists allow Nashville, their manager, agent, or record label to change them in the hopes of achieving greater fame and fortune. If they do morph into what they were coached to become, it usually serves to alienate them from their previously existing audience, and their "newfound success" is usually short lived because it's not coming from a place of authenticity.

Loba and BBR Music Group are incredibly successful because they don't attempt to change the artist; they allow the artists to be their authentic selves. BBR serves to amplify their artists' message.

Bru

Authenticity is not only important in the music industry; I quickly learned its value as an entrepreneur. In 2007, shortly after I began my career as a speaker and author, I was told by a marketing and image consultant to ditch my jeans and boots for a suit. She said my clothing looked weird, and I should also change the way I spoke and the appearance of my marketing collateral. If I didn't fit in, she said, I didn't stand a chance of succeeding. I made the mistake Loba mentioned and I let the industry change me.

I found it didn't help—it actually hurt my results. I wound up having to compete for business because I wasn't attracting business by simply being my authentic self. Shortly thereafter, I ditched the herd mentality and returned to the world of suits wearing my boots; I made my website, marketing materials, and message reflect my authentic self. Like Domino's business after its pizza makeover, my revenue grew; and like Eldredge, when I shared my own struggles with my audiences, not only did my message improve but their response did too. Weird, how that works.

Brett Eldredge's Twitter profile reads, "Step into the weirdness." The weirdness he refers to is actually authenticity. What makes authenticity weird is simply that so many brands don't practice it. Ninety-eight percent fail at authenticity, according to my friend Rick Barker, author of the *Music Industry Blueprint*. Barker's philosophy is that "weird wins." He explained that 98 percent of the population won't do what it takes to succeed authentically because it feels weird. He believes that if you are willing to get weird, you eliminate 98 percent of your competition. Step into your weirdness, it's your competitive advantage.

Opting for a Silverado instead of a limo is weird? A drummer playing without drumsticks is weird? Advertising that is critical of your own pizza is weird? Or just maybe we aren't weird enough? Step into your weirdness—it's your competitive advantage.

You

What are you sharing with your customers that enables them to see and applaud your human side? It could be owning your mistakes and publicly declaring you're on a mission to fix them, like Domino's Pizza did with its initiative. Perhaps, like Granger Smith, it's insisting on representing your brand in a manner that is 100 percent congruent with your core values. Channel your inner Alan Jackson by rejecting the notion that you should script or fake what you're doing for the sake of convenience and public perception.

Ronald Reagan was an actor, as stadium status as they got during his era, but when he left Hollywood and became president of the United States he refused to wear makeup for television appearances. His chief of staff, Michael Deaver, once asked Reagan to take off his blazer and sling it over his shoulder for a photograph. Reagan insisted he couldn't do that because that's not his authentic self and the public would know because the camera never lies.

In another famous exchange between Deaver and Reagan, a fan approached them on the streets of New York City, handed Reagan a pen and paper, and said, "Wow, I always wanted to meet the actor Ray Milland. Can I please have your autograph, Mr. Milland?" Reagan smiled and signed the paper as Ray Milland. As they walked away, Deaver questioned Reagan about why he didn't tell the man who he really was. Reagan responded by saying, "Why? I know who I am." Think about this for a minute: an actor turned politician was adamant about authenticity and transparency.

This begs the question, do you know who you are? I think we are all in these stories. Our success is ultimately about our ability to put people at ease while being comfortable in our own skin. We can reject the "scripts" of the business world, the photo shoots with fake settings inserted as background. Sadly, in the era of Photoshop, Auto-Tune, and high-tech video editing, examples are a dime a dozen and only serve to cheapen a brand's value. Do yourself and your brand a favor and insist on keeping it real. The public's trust in you will only rise as a result.

Stadium Steps

1. Get weird. What is one thing about you or your business that is so dramatically different from everyone else in your industry that they would all label it as weird?
   (When you can answer that, you've probably found your biggest competitive advantage.)
2. Step into that weirdness by being real with your audience and getting personal in order to better connect with them. What would that look like for you?
3. Present yourself precisely as you are. You don't need an image consultant or a focus group to tell you what to do. You are your own person, equipped with your own compass. It will point you in the right direction.
4. Use self-deprecating humor. Having the courage and vulnerability to allow people to laugh with you and at you will show your authenticity and quickly win people over.

CHAPTER 6

Your Ego Is Not Your Amigo

Sometimes I am two people. Johnny is the nice one. Cash causes all the trouble.
They fight.

—Johnny Cash

Clark Kent has Superman, Bruce Wayne has Batman, John Brubaker has Coach Morgan Randall, and Granger Smith has Earl Dibbles Jr. Country music star Granger Smith is curator of one of pop culture's most beloved alter egos.

alter ego (noun): a different version of yourself.

The right alter ego can be a personal launch point that helps you grow your platform and expand your brand to stadium status. Earl did that for Smith, as the growth of Smith's platform enabled him to move from long-time independent artist to signing a deal with Broken Bow Records. To help you grow to stadium status, I encourage you to take a page out of Smith's playbook and create an alter ego for yourself.

Your ego is not your amigo. It causes you to hold back and not take chances because it's human nature to worry about eight deadly words: What will others think? What will others say? The problem is that holding back never produced great results.

It's a normal feeling and, according to Smith, "Every artist and entrepreneur has a box they typically have to work in. Having an alter ego allows you to not only think outside the box but work outside that box as well."

If you're an introvert (about half the population is), an alter ego gives you the freedom to become a bigger, bolder version of yourself. Even if you're naturally extraverted (like me), you can utilize an alter ego to drive your message home in an over-the-top and even more entertaining way.

Them

What began as a humorous YouTube video that went viral evolved into Smith's alter ego recording songs and videos and appearing as an encore act at his concerts. Earl Dibbles Jr., the brand, has evolved to the point where he (not Granger Smith) is a featured analyst on CBS Sports, picking the college football games of the week.

"Evolved" is the key word. Smith explained that he didn't set out to create an alter ego all at once. "Every aspect of Earl grew organically by listening to the fans and what they said they wanted," Smith said. The tangible benefits for Smith have been elevated audience engagement, brand expansion, new revenue streams, and increased media attention. The right alter ego can connect your brand to a broader audience.

Here's why it works. Earl Dibbles Jr. is an unfiltered outlet that lets Granger say whatever he wants. An alter ego can give you creative license, as well, when your real personality might not be able to get away with saying and doing certain things. The character is authentic and relatable because everyone can envision an Earl Dibbles in their life or family. The proof is in the numbers; Smith's social media following has been eclipsed by his alter ego's, but the beauty is that both contribute to the same brand platform.

When I asked Smith about his famous alter ego, he likened Earl to McDonalds's McRib sandwich. When McDonald's launched the McRib, it would sell the sandwich for a short period of time and take it away to gauge customer response before expanding the sandwich's presence. That is precisely how Smith's alter ego grew to include his own songs, videos, and merchandise.

Bru

Following a playbook similar to Smith's, I created my alter ego, Coach Morgan Randall, who is modeled after the central character in my book *Seeds of Success*. The book has been adapted into a screenplay and is in the process of becoming a major motion picture. Using an alter ego to expand the brand and bring the central character to life in some entertaining ways has helped drive book sales, build a following in advance of the movie's release, and generate revenue.

Coach Randall is the ultimate paradox: philosophical yet simple and serious yet playful, he serves as a wise, old mentor who doesn't take himself so seriously that he can't learn from the younger generations around him. What originally began as a Twitter account, @TheCoachRandall quickly amassed more than 100,000 followers (eclipsing my own account), gained media attention, and, like Earl Dibbles Jr., has grown into a brand unto itself. There is now a website, CoachMorganRandall.com, which provides access to the character on all social media platforms and features a line of branded merchandise for sale.

To echo the sentiments of Granger Smith, my alter ego grew organically based on feedback from readers and fans. The brand even drew the interest of an apparel company and led us to partner on a line of Coach Morgan Randall–branded apparel.

Coach Randall's standard attire is a T-shirt, a coach's whistle worn around his neck, a varsity jacket, and old-school black cleats with bleach-white laces.

When he is required to dress up, you will find him in a green argyle sports coat, jeans, and white suede shoes. When I'm hired to speak about *Seeds of Success* I dress in the argyle blazer and portray a bull-in-a-china-shop edginess that is uncharacteristic of John Brubaker. It's part of the persona that's really required to get the message across. Coach Randall always projects a sort of odd-man-out personality and takes pride in standing out. It's important for me to walk my talk because I encourage other leaders to embrace the odd-man-out personality type and feel comfortable standing out. When I put on the blazer and get in character as Coach Morgan Randall, it's like I'm an athlete putting his uniform on: it's game time and I am going to go perform and compete. My friends and family like to refer to the transformation as me getting into "coach mode." Quite simply, transforming into an alter ego allows you to play the game in a different way and at a different level.

There is also a huge intangible benefit a lot of people don't see. An alter ego enables you to compartmentalize your work from your personal life. Just like entertainers, we entrepreneurs are on stage in our businesses, but much of life is lived off stage in the company of family and friends. We are not, and should not be, the same person at home that we are in the office or on the stage. We all have two selves: our work self and our home self. How do you shift into high gear at work and then downshift and be truly present at home? I would argue that you do so with an alter ego.

So who should you be dressing to impress when you transform into your alter ego? Yourself. Research indicates that what we wear affects not just other people's perceptions of us but our self-perception as well. The concept is known as embodied cognition, and it refers to the fact that our physical appearances and experiences affect the way we think as much as our brains do.

In a 2012 article, "Unclothed Cognition," published in the *Journal of Experimental Social Psychology,* researchers Hajo Adam and Adam Galinsky discussed their findings that participants who wore a white lab coat that they believed belonged to a doctor were more focused. The participants who wore the same white coat but were told it belonged to a painter scored significantly lower on the attention test. Something as simple as believing a white coat belonged to a doctor rather than a painter helped participants spot the differences in two pictures placed side by side.

This study offers a compelling reason that you need to dress the part when it comes to your alter ego. There's an old saying in sports: "Look good, feel good, play good." As the research indicates, this adage holds true in the workplace as well. Dress to impress yourself.

You

If you're scratching your head about how to construct an alter ego or are wondering where to begin, worry no more. Don't overthink it, and let the game come to you. There are, however a few things to consider. Here's how to create your alter ego:

- Determine why you want an alter ego. Your "character" could be as simple as a pen name or alias, or as complex as a completely different persona.
- Decide on the personality of your alter ego. Does he or she show up as a super-sized, more confident version of yourself? Earl is larger than life and completely unapologetic, which is precisely why people embrace him.
- Create a distinct image. Earl Dibbles Jr. contrasts greatly with Granger Smith. While Smith has an everyday good ol' country boy image, his Earl persona is so over the top that people laugh and view it as a parody of a stereotypical beer-drinking, tobacco-chewing, truck-driving country boy.
- Come up with your alter ego's origin story. Make sure it differs from yours. Where did he (or she) come from? How is he shaped by his unique past, like you're shaped by yours?
- Remember that everything's in the name. Granger Smith gave his alter ego the name Earl Dibbles Jr. because he believes it resonates, as everyone knows someone just like Earl. Smith shared with me that he has relatives who are just like Dibbles, which makes it easy to get into character. Dibbles is a huge departure from a surname as common as Smith. Plus, you have to admit, the name Earl Dibbles Jr. is about as country as it gets.
- Highlight contradictions. Like the bull in the china shop that is Coach Randall and the more polished professional that is John Brubaker, you and your alter ego should be the ultimate paradox, from the names to the appearance, quirky personality traits, and idiosyncrasies. When done well, your alter ego should present a walking, talking contradiction to your own persona.
- Create a uniform. Clark Kent changed into tights and a cape inside a phone booth. Coach Morgan Randall sports an argyle blazer, and Earl Dibbles Jr. wears a white tank, overalls, and work boots. What sort of uniform will your alter ego don? Make it memorable, and it will become part of your brand.

Stadium Steps

1. Purchase the domain name that belongs to your alter ego.
2. Create matching social media accounts and get active on them.
3. Treat the entire process like a social science experiment.

   a. Float your ideas, content, products, or services out there in cyberspace or real life. Are you easing new products or services into the market instead of forcing something you want that customers might not?

b. Measure your audience's response to your offering.

c. Tweak your offering slightly and test this second version against the first. Keep whichever works better.

d. Interact and engage your audience. Ask them questions and respond promptly (and thoughtfully) to their questions.

e. Incorporate your audience's feedback and suggestions into your alter ego's brand.

f. Listen carefully to your fans; they will tell you everything you need to know in order to grow. Audiences always do.

4. Have fun with your alter ego. If it feels like work, you're doing it wrong. It's supposed to be playful and entertaining, not just for your customers but also for you and your team.

PART II

Execution

CHAPTER 7

Everyone Recruits

It's impossible to simply manufacture talent, you have to recruit it.
—Coach Bru

In my past career, I was a college lacrosse coach for twelve years. It looks glamorous, until you get a peek behind the scenes. In short, 90 percent of a coach's success is recruiting. It's the lifeblood of any program. What people don't realize is that recruiting wins games way more than X's and O's ever will. Coaches are constantly recruiting. If you're not recruiting student-athletes, you're recruiting boosters, and if you're not recruiting boosters, you're recruiting fans.

Years ago, my mentor introduced me to a concept called RDOP, which stands for "recruit daily or perish." When I first became a head coach I was essentially a staff of one and responsible for all the recruiting. As my staff grew over the years I became more like a CEO and found myself managing more and recruiting less.

If you've moved out of start-up mode this probably sounds quite familiar. I called my mentor one time to complain about the state of affairs my team was in, and he asked a simple question: "What did you do to build your program today?" I didn't have an intelligent answer.

It was at this time that I made the promise to myself that, no matter how busy I was or where my travels took me, I would recruit daily. Even if some days that meant only making one recruiting call, it became a nonnegotiable. (My wife was less than impressed when I called my top prospect from the delivery room of the hospital shortly before our daughter was born.)

You don't have to be a coach to recruit. Everybody recruits. Coaches recruit athletes, firms recruit employees, salespeople recruit clients, and entrepreneurs recruit investors. If you're not recruiting daily, don't be surprised that you're not getting the results you want.

Living by the motto of "recruit daily or perish" made my college lacrosse program grow. When I retired from coaching and became the manager of an

ESPN Radio affiliate, that attitude made our revenue grow. Fast-forward to today, and it has made my business grow.

Recruiting is about engaging an audience. If you want a bigger or better audience, you want to learn how to engage. All the world's a stage, and we are all players, to borrow the words of Shakespeare. On stage and off, musicians recruit. They recruit record labels to sign them, fans to listen to them, radio stations to play their music, and sponsors to support them. Whether you realize it or not, you recruit too. You're a recruiter first, and you're whatever your job title might be second. In athletics, your ability to recruit is even more important than your ability to coach. I would argue that is the case in every other industry as well. Without recruits, there's no one to buy your product or service, rendering it useless.

Them

Like a CEO, director of human resources, executive search recruiter, or even a college coach, record label executives are in the business of talent acquisition. The great ones possess the ability to mine for diamonds. Great recruiters see things in prospects that others don't, and often they see things that the prospect doesn't even see in himself.

Jon Loba, executive vice president of BBR Music Group, is one of the best recruiters you'll find in any industry. He just happens to work in country music. Jon's forte is mining for diamonds.

After being dropped by Capital Records, Jason Aldean was ready to pack it in and head back home to Georgia. Then he performed a showcase at the Wild Horse Saloon, and attending that night were Jon Loba and Benny Brown of BBR Music Group. BBR's stable of musicians was full and Loba didn't have any intentions of signing another artist, especially not one who had recently been dropped by another label. But he saw something in Aldean that no one else did, and they signed him on the spot. Loba's instincts were right: all five of Aldean's albums have been certified platinum. He's also the digitally best-selling male country artist in history.

Aldean was the first male country act of his generation to achieve stadium status, as he's headlined stadiums from Georgia's Sanford Stadium to Boston's iconic Fenway Park, as well as multiple other Major League Baseball stadiums.

Some recruiters catch lightning in a bottle once, but that isn't the case with Loba. He also saw something special in other artists he signed. Dustin Lynch's future with Valory Music Co. was uncertain, so Loba, on behalf of BBR, orchestrated the musical equivalent of sports free agency—Lynch was under contract with Valory Music Co., an imprint of Big Machine Label Group, and Loba offered Big Machine a percentage of Lynch's future earnings in exchange for the rights to sign him to BBR. Lynch had his first chart-topping song shortly thereafter, and his star has been on the rise ever since.

After fifteen years of trying to make it to the big time, husband and wife duo Thompson Square were ready to hang it up and leave Nashville. On a whim, they performed one last showcase, and that's where Jon Loba discovered them. After signing with BBR, Thompson Square has enjoyed two hit albums and as many number-one singles.

Another coup to BBR's credit is the resurgence of Randy Houser's career. The artist had already spent time on three other labels before finding a home at BBR. His singles "How Country Feels" and "We Went" both rose to the number-one spot on the charts.

CEOs and business owners often lament that "we just don't have enough talent on our team," or, when they are hiring, that "there isn't a deep enough pool of talent to choose from." I couldn't disagree more. We don't have a talent problem in our workforce, we have a confidence problem. There's an abundance of employees with potential, but without confidence their potential doesn't stand a chance of being transformed into performance. This is why a culture of workplace coaching plays such a critical role: coaches and recruiters see talent in us that we don't see in ourselves. They're in the transformation business. Great coaches tell you what you don't want to hear and get you to do what you don't think you can so you can become something you didn't think you could become. Whenever I see this happen, whether it's in business, music, or sports, I'm reminded of the fact that confidence is king. It's the one thing that affects all things.

Bru

Sometimes, reminders come from unlikely sources. On Saturdays, my kids and I go horseback riding. One Saturday their coach, Jen, was out of town, so her teenage daughter Hannah filled in and taught my kids. My oldest daughter, Meredith, is an experienced rider, and Hannah knows her well, having seen her compete in shows.

My younger child, Julia, on the other hand, isn't a known quantity to Hannah. Julia is very much a novice and, unbeknownst to Hannah, she hasn't jumped or even cantered. Julia is not the most confident kid and tends to proceed with caution in everything she does.

The interesting thing about confidence is that it's contagious. When you're low on confidence you can borrow it from other people who possess it in abundance. Hannah is one of those people—she's fearless on a horse. This rubbed off on Julia in a big way, and that day she jumped with no fear and handled a cranky horse's attitude with confidence.

More importantly, there was a huge carryover effect. After the lesson, you could see Julia's walk replaced by a swagger, and her tone of voice even reflected this confidence boost. Days later, it has spilled over into her schoolwork and still hasn't worn off. She left the stables that day transformed.

We are all in this story. We all have the ability to transform the employees, prospects, clients, and customers we serve on a daily basis. That hour Hannah spent with Julia was a lesson in the power of the Pygmalion Effect, the tendency of people to perform to the level others expect of them. It's named for Pygmalion, a character in Ovid's narrative poem *Metamorphoses*; a sculptor, Pygmalion could look at a slab of marble and see the sculpture inside it.

In 1968, psychologist Robert Rosenthal did a research study in which elementary school students were given a disguised IQ test. Their scores were not disclosed to teachers. Teachers were told that some of their students (about 20 percent, chosen at random) could be expected to be high achievers that year, performing better than expected in comparison to their classmates. These high achievers' names were shared with the teachers.

At the end of the study, all students were given the same IQ test used at the beginning of the study. While all students showed an improvement in IQ when retested at the end of the study, the students labeled high achievers scored significantly better than the others. These "high achievers" were in fact ordinary students—the teachers had been misled by Rosenthal.

The Pygmalion Effect explains why our relationships tend to be self-fulfilling prophecies. A self-fulfilling prophecy is the belief that something will come true, and as a result of the belief it does indeed come true. For example, if you don't believe someone can perform at a high level, you will always find reasons why this is true. If you believe someone isn't good enough (perhaps that someone might even be yourself), that lack of confidence will show up consistently and kill your results because you will act in a way that affirms your belief. When you've set expectations for someone, high or low, the person will tend to live up to those expectations. This isn't limited to the classroom; it plays out every day in boardrooms and meeting rooms as well. And on the fateful Saturday of Julia's horseback riding lesson, I was reminded of two of the most important factors in success:

1. You've got to believe strongly in others before you can lead them.
2. The strength of your belief in others has the ability to overcome their disbelief in themselves.

The lesson for you as a leader is that you don't want to be in the transaction business, you want to be in the transformation business. Your clients arrive one way, and after their experience with you they leave transformed, a better version of themselves.

Be warned, though: the Pygmalion Effect doesn't warrant unrealistic expectations of your people. Hoping for a miracle is not an effective leadership strategy.

You

I hope perhaps you saw a little bit of yourself in the stories of artists before Jon Loba signed them, or maybe in the example with my daughter Julia. Regardless of what you're seeing or feeling, there's one thing you absolutely cannot do: quit. I'm begging you not to give up on your goals. No matter how hopeless your situation might seem or how far ahead your competition may be, you can overcome the obstacles if you persist.

Your career is a lot like a musician's; it's a marathon, not a sprint, and you just don't know when your opportunity may come. You need to trust the process and realize that, as you are building a body of work, others will see things in you that you can't see in yourself. After all, you can't see the picture when you're trapped inside the frame.

The stories you just read are all huge come-from-behind victories. Your career, like those of the musicians I featured, is a game that can be won not just by skill but by will. These musicians just didn't give up, they didn't stop believing, even when there was lots of evidence that might have persuaded them that they should. Whether you're a music fan or not, there is a huge lesson you can learn from these artists: it pays to finish strong.

Even when it seems like there is no hope, one conversation, one phone call, one client, or one sale can turn things around in your favor if you apply these takeaways from each of the BBR musicians.

Jason Aldean takeaway: Keep the faith, stay the course, and commit your-self in full measure until there's no time left on the clock.

Dustin Lynch takeaway: When one door appears to be closing, another opens. Move through the open doors that present themselves to you. Sometimes change is disguised as opportunity.

Thompson Square takeaway: One event can make all the difference. Encour-age your teammates to maintain their discipline, know their role, and pay attention to details.

Randy Houser takeaway: Timing, fit, and entry point matter in all industries. While you may not initially find yourself in the right place at the right time, keep the faith that a better fit, where your true value is embraced, may reveal itself later.

Five Reasons to RDOP

Make the promise to recruit daily. It will do these five things for your business:

1. *Reinforce purpose.* Why are you in business? To make sales and raise revenue. Sales are the points on your scoreboard, and committing to that nonnegotiable daily activity reinforces your purpose. I keep a personal scoreboard and make sure I'm making twenty contacts a day, no matter what.

2. *Dominate focus.* When your employees see you "recruiting" daily or see you publicly praising the custodian for keeping the facility spot-less to make a better first impression on prospective clients, it's like the shot heard 'round the company. Everyone quickly understands

recruiting is mission critical at all levels of the company and must be everyone's dominant focus. Everyone recruits, even the custodian and the groundskeeper.

3. *Keep your finger on the pulse.* If you don't recruit daily, you lose touch with your customer base (I don't care if you have a sales manager, you need to get out there too). It's market research, public relations, and client retention all rolled into one. Customers will tell the owner things they won't tell the salesperson. I've seen it happen time and time again with clients.

4. *Move from adversity to advantage.* Getting rejected out on the road or over the phone can help you discover new solutions and creative opportunities.

5. *Accelerate growth.* Plain and simple, growth is what every entrepreneur is seeking by the ton. Recruiting daily is like an insurance policy to prevent perishing in your business. I have coaching clients complain all the time that their salespeople are underperforming. My first recommendation is to go walk a mile in their shoes before we discuss the matter again.

Going on the road with your sales reps gives you a lot of windshield time to talk to them, get to know them better, and understand the unique challenges they face. It also enables you to help them make more sales. In the process, you'll find that their jobs are not as easy as you think.

How do you reinforce RDOP? Advertise it, to yourself and to your entire company, so that it creates top-of-mind awareness. I have RDOP printed on my screen saver, iPhone case, dashboard, and landline receiver. It's become a reminder I can't avoid seeing, no matter where I go.

Stadium Steps

1. Let me begin by asking you the same question my mentor asked me: what did you do to grow your business today? (You need to be able to answer this question at day's end, every single day.)
2. What are you expecting from people who work for and with you?
3. Are you sure you're setting the bar high enough?
4. Are you consistently serving as a confidence giver with your clients?
5. What would you attempt today if you knew you absolutely couldn't fail?

CHAPTER 8

No Small Stages

All the world's a stage.

—William Shakespeare

When you look at the paths taken to stadium status stardom, a common theme emerges: no stage is too small and there's no linear route to success. That can be said for entertainers, athletes, and entrepreneurs alike. Country musician and 2013 *Celebrity Apprentice* winner Trace Adkins was performing one night at a tiny country bar in Mount Juliet, outside of Nashville, when the president of Capitol Records saw him and offered him a recording contract. Martina McBride was discovered while selling merchandise for Garth Brooks on his tour in the early 1990s. Brooks was so impressed with her voice that he asked her to become his opening act, and she went on to stardom as a headliner herself.

In 1971 Oprah Winfrey won Nashville's Ms. Fire Prevention contest and went to the radio station to claim her prize. While she was there, the station manager invited her on air for a segment. He fell in love with her voice and offered her a position to read the news on air. The Oprah dynasty began with an audience of one in what wasn't even intended to be an audition.

Them

Often, the teacher becomes the student. This happened to me, at one of those times when it was just what I needed when I needed it. One summer Saturday I learned a valuable lesson from Trevor Laliberte, a young musician who is a former student of mine. He was invited to perform at an outdoor music festival in downtown Portland. There were multiple stages set up all over the Old Port section of the city, and the weather was supposed to be perfect for an outdoor summer concert. However, in typical New England fashion, it began to rain and the concert was a virtual rainout. All musicians using electric guitars and amps were told they wouldn't be able to perform due to the weather, but those who played acoustic instruments, like Trevor Laliberte, could still perform. To say the weather kept the crowd away would be an understatement. Trevor performed under a small tent in the park, and his audience consisted of a handful of passersby and homeless people scattered about the lawn.

I couldn't have been more impressed with the young man's professionalism. Many teenagers in his shoes would have either not shown up or mailed it in, so to speak, and simply not given their all. Not Laliberte, though. He brought the same energy he would have if he were performing in a sold-out stadium. When I asked him about the experience Laliberte told me, "We need to take every opportunity to put ourselves out there because, chances are, you're going to leave an impression on at least one person, and one person can make all the difference."

That's not just true for musicians; it's wisdom we should all follow in business. His advice and example were also the timely reminder I needed. Two days later I was scheduled to speak in New York City to an association of executives. The meeting planner told me there would be a large audience, but on the night of the event the final headcount turned out to be just thirty-five. After speaking at three national conventions in jam-packed convention centers in the weeks before, a small room of thirty-five people was a letdown—until I remembered Trevor Laliberte's words of wisdom, that is.

Me

In 1997, my first year as a head coach, I was hired so late in the year that I didn't have much time to recruit for the upcoming season. When I went to recruiting events, I felt like the last guy in the buffet line at the cafeteria . . . nothing left but crumbs. I was bitter, dejected, and disheartened, and I felt like I'd gotten myself into a hopeless situation. I wanted to be a head coach, so I took an undesirable job and had been dealt a tough hand. As time went on, I found that the crumbs I had on my team that year had tremendous value. While short in stature (and talent), they were connectors. A group of likeable guys, they had deep networks and created referrals for me that enabled us to build a strong recruiting class the following year. I appreciated those crumbs and learned a valuable lesson: when you serve the crumbs well, they turn into a feast.

Crumb appreciation has served me well professionally. It has enabled me to build a successful consulting and speaking business 100 percent by referral—no advertising, no cold calls, no gimmicks.

In October 2009, one of my colleagues referred me to what would be my first client, a small nonprofit in Northern New England. The group wanted a peak performance workshop but had a very small budget, and the audience was a whopping one dozen people packed into a small room that masqueraded as a cafeteria. Twelve years later, I was back in a cafeteria and getting nothing but crumbs!

Only this time, thanks to my recruiting experience, I was wise enough to be grateful for those crumbs and to the person who referred them to me. I discounted my fee to fit their budget, I overdelivered on the content, and I am still in touch with those twelve crumbs. They are a blessing, and have referred me to some of my best coaching clients and to numerous consulting and speaking engagements, and they've been some of the biggest champions of my books and other projects. I've done work for that nonprofit for eight years now, and its budget has grown; and as that budget has grown, my loyalty and generosity have been rewarded. Furthermore, some of the best friends I've made came from that crumb client.

My practice in this instance flies in the face of the advice many experts will give you. Lots of experts incorrectly told me:

- "Only target the wealthiest prospects that can pay you a premium."
- "Never, ever discount your fee."
- "You should only be speaking in major venues."
- "You must have a major publisher for your book."

I'm glad I didn't listen to any of them. There are no absolutes like that in any industry, and history has proven that my model works. It's something I learned from sports. Sometimes the biggest plays come from capitalizing on the smallest opportunities (the crumbs and the smallest audiences). In my coaching career I've seen a loose ball turn into a game-winning goal, a simple catch and run that killed a penalty, and a shot deflect off my goalie's glove to seal an overtime victory. It's why sport is a metaphor for life: each is a game of inches. Little things win big games, and when you serve small opportunities well they become big opportunities.

There are no small stages, just people who choose to play small. I recently had a client who hired me to coach her on building her consulting and speaking business. She said she was frustrated because she couldn't find "the right clients" or "a major platform." I don't think this was the case. She was focused on finding big-time clients and being on the biggest stage. What she didn't realize was that her current clients are her big-time clients, her major platform is her front porch, and the next person who walks past is her audience. She just needed to learn how to catch the ball and run hard. It's what we all need to do. When you master those things, opportunities will present themselves.

You

Are you thinking like my client was thinking? People make the mistake of looking only for big opportunities, or, worse yet, expecting the finished product to come to them. Life and business don't work that way, and these people wind up missing the little things that make a big difference. Focus on your fundamentals, and execute the right technique—these are the little things. You will never do big things until you do small things in a big way. In business, you don't receive a feast, you receive crumbs. If you don't see that the feast is actually in the crumbs, you'll mistakenly throw away the crumbs and starve as you keep wishing for the feast to come to you.

Some may say chance encounters and timing are just luck. I prefer to think that luck favors the prepared. To truly be prepared, we need to consistently show up and bring our best, whether we are in front of an audience of 35, 350, 3500, 35,000, or a stadium of 135,000. Nobody knows what the "one big break" will be until after it happens.

There is no linear route to entrepreneurial success. It is a long and winding road, so the best thing we can all do is suspend judgment and commit ourselves in full measure to what we are doing. You will suffer disappointments and setbacks but you must maintain your hope and confidence. The lesson for all of us is that we need to live our lives as good examples because we never know who is watching or who we affect—and it only takes one person to change things.

Every headliner was once an opening act and every major leaguer spent time in the minor leagues. There's no such thing as a small stage, so go play your music for the fans in your audience who want to hear it.

Stadium Steps

1. List three crumbs that you've currently been minimizing instead of maximizing.
2. How can you better show "crumb appreciation" for them and turn those crumbs into a feast?
3. What's one thing you can do to put yourself out there and make a positive impression, even if it's just on one person?

CHAPTER 9

Game Changer

You're either staying the same or changing the game.

—Coach Bru

Like entertainers, we businesspeople are all performers. Our office just looks a little different. And like us, entertainers are entrepreneurs. Their industries are incredibly cutthroat, volatile, and unpredictable. I'm sure you can relate.

According to the SBA (Small Business Administration), 30 percent of small businesses fail to survive more than two years and almost half fail within the first five years. That's a walk in the park compared with the stats in the music industry. According to Vinny Ribas, CEO of Nashville-based artist management firm Indie Connect, the success rate of the musician is much worse than that of the business owner. This is evidenced by the fact that Nashville is what he calls "a five-year town," meaning that's how long it takes to begin to build relationships and trust in the music industry.

On any given night, three hundred to four hundred musicians are performing live in Nashville. How do you compete in that market? If you're smart, you don't. Instead, you create something so one of a kind and compelling that you create a "market of one," which you own. In my interview with Ribas, I learned that the way you make it big in business is exactly the same way you make it big in the music industry. He indicated that, "The key to success at the highest level is that you must bring something different. Do this and you have a huge advantage."

The epitome of different would have to be rapping cowboy Troy Coleman, aka Cowboy Troy, who invented "hick hop" (country rap) music. Tripp Lee, too, defines "different"; aka DJ Sinister, he doesn't just spin regular dance tracks but mixes in country music with hip hop beats. In an incredibly homogenous genre, these musicians made names for themselves by standing out in a sea of sameness. You owe it to yourself to take a page out of their playbook because you're either different or you're invisible in your industry too.

A lot of experts throw around the buzzwords "niching" and "best practices." When it comes to positioning your brand, ditch these tired old buzzwords.

Everybody is niching so it's not unique, and the problem with best practices is that they are common practices. The term I use when discussing positioning with clients is the same term I use to describe Cowboy Troy and DJ Sinister: game changer.

game changer (noun): a person, event, or process that effects a significant shift in the current method of competing.

Being a game changer is about doing things in a way that's never been done before and as a result elevating and separating yourself from the competition. Why is this advantageous? The best practice (pardon the pun) is to be nontraditional and create new demand via a completely new experience. When you do this, you create a market of one for yourself. It's the best way to stand out in any industry. Sadly, many entrepreneurs buy into a certain groupthink that prevents them from ever becoming a category unto themselves. When your prospects can easily compare you to competitors, you've probably already lost, because if you've been compared you've been commoditized. They view you as one of many, not one of a kind, and the only differentiator then becomes price. You get forced into a race to the bottom because you haven't positioned yourself as one of a kind in the eyes of your clients.

How do you make a name for yourself in a crowded, hypercompetitive industry? By not competing. There isn't a lot of space to operate where it's crowded, so you need to position yourself in a place where you own the space.

In every industry there are people playing the game and then there are the rare few, like Troy and Tripp, who are changing the game. Players all try to compete on the same field; game changers, on the other hand, create a whole new field they get to own. This strategy is essentially redefining the boundaries by breaking them.

How to Be a Game Changer

So how do you change the game? To quote Tripp, "Listen to the market; the market never lies." He started to deejay and mix beats with country music to bring a new energy to live Big & Rich shows in the form of a twenty- to thirty-minute warm-up for the crowd. It was something the audience had never experienced before, and they responded well. This real-time reaction is how he knew he was on to something. Radio program directors started requesting to put his content on the radio. What began with air time on one station in Chicago turned into a syndicated show, Country Fried Mix, in thirty markets across the United States.

How can you elevate the energy level of your audience? What live events could feed your business online?

"Not just ahead of the curve, you set the curve and everyone follows what you did." These were the words that Laura Coleman, Cowboy Troy's wife, used when describing his game-changing approach. His core values remain the same today as they were when he began in 2001: make music fun for himself and fun for his friends and audiences. In the process, he invented and trademarked the term Hick Hop well before country music began incorporating rap elements. Other artists distanced themselves from the term, thinking they needed to fit in to gain acceptance in the industry. Coleman knew better, and has been unapologetic about embracing the description even when people viewed him as a novelty early on. As a result, his brand has taken off. To quote Coleman, the takeaway for us is that "in business, people vote with their wallets," which speaks to the authenticity consumers are seeking from brands.

Are you setting the curve while maintaining a sense of fun? How might being unapologetically authentic about your brand boost your business? Your goal should be to do in your industry what the cowboy and the DJ have done in their genre: provide something for clients that they just can't get anywhere else. The key is to have your clients buy *you*, not merely your service or product. Sure, your product is part of the total package, but bigger than the product itself is the brand that is uniquely and exclusively you. Be different or be invisible.

If you're not different, you're going to be lumped in with the many others who do what you do. But simply being different is not enough. You need to help people connect the dots between who you are and what you do by gaining and maintaining their attention.

The biggest problem you have isn't the competition, undercapitalization, lousy margins, bad employees, poor lead generation, or lack of investors; it's obscurity. In other words, you just don't have enough people paying attention to your brand, product, or service.

Attention comes first; then you can monetize people's attention. It's incredibly hard to gain people's attention, much less maintain it. Why? Because it's hard to get people to stop what they are doing, look up, and take notice. But you need to make getting attention a priority because, in most cases, very few people have a clear idea of who you are and why you should matter to them. It's not your fault; bigger and long-standing brands own the majority of the market share in your space.

The obscurity of your brand may reveal itself in one or more of the following scenarios:

- Most people have never heard of your brand.
- People may know who you are but have no idea what you do.
- Maybe they've heard of you and have a loose idea of what you do but they don't fully or accurately understand your offering.
- Then there is always a small core of people who know you well and know exactly the value you bring.

The bottom line is that you may have great value, but people have to be able to find you. There are very few professions in which you can simply hang up a shingle and have people come find you. In Maine, we have a saying that the fish won't come to you, you have to go to the fish. In business, it behooves us to fish in stocked ponds and bait multiple hooks. How many hooks? Seven!

The Law of Sevens

It's a widely held philosophy that seven is a lucky number. There are seven days in a week, Seven Wonders of the World, seven deadly sins, seven notes on the musical scale, seven colors in a rainbow, seven continents, seven seas, and seventh heaven. When it comes to your brand, seven isn't so much a lucky number as it is the minimum number of attention-gaining "hooks" or methods you need to employ to solve your problems. Our brains remember things in units of seven, phone numbers, for example. Simply put, seven is the right size for a highly effective memory chunk or cognitive load.

Them

Troy Coleman, aka Cowboy Troy, the inventor of Hick Hop, shared his application of the law of sevens with me in an interview. Coleman is incredibly well branded nationally and internationally, yet sometimes folks still have trouble connecting the dots. Here are Coleman's multiple lines in stocked ponds:

1. Hosts *Nashville Star* on USA Network;
2. Tours with Big & Rich;
3. Tours nationally performing solo shows;
4. Appears as one of the faces of the ESPN College Gameday Theme Song;
5. Appears frequently as a guest on sports talk shows;
6. Maintains strong social media presence and insightful blog;
7. Has music on radio, YouTube, Spotify, Pandora, iTunes.

It's fairly simple for a recording artist to produce music, but the music is just the starting point, not the end point, when it comes to people's awareness. Case in point, television is the most powerful medium in the United States, turning some show hosts into household names. Yet people still needed other prompts to connect Troy and his music beyond simply knowing he hosted the television program *Nashville Star*. If someone with Troy's level of visibility on national television needs other means of connecting the dots for people, what should make us think we are any different?

Bru

I know that in today's age of digital distraction, if all an author does is write a book he won't ever be a household name. (That said, my kids are tweens, so right now I'm not even a household name in my own household.) Clients are attracted to me via several points of reference beyond my books. For me, these are just a starting point and the list doesn't even include my blog, weekly newsletter, membership site, social media presence, and "Coach Bru Tube" which is the YouTube channel for my brand.

My seven points of reference:

1. Author
2. Radio show host
3. Magazine columnist
4. Podcast host
5. Executive coach
6. Professional speaker
7. Media guest.

We all have to bring our brand to life in a variety of ways because people's learning styles differ. The three primary learning styles people tend to employ are visual, auditory, and kinesthetic, commonly referred to as the VAK model. Roughly a third of the population are visual learners, another third are auditory learners, and the final third are kinesthetic learners. People with a visual learning style will retain information best by reading, watching videos, or looking at pictures, infographs, charts, and diagrams. Auditory learners prefer lectures, podcasts, audiobooks, music, stories told aloud, and discussion. The methods that best resonate with kinesthetic learners are role playing, interactive exercises, and hands-on activities. These varied learning styles are the reason I bring my brand to life utilizing all of the VAK components in my seven areas of reference. Using *Stadium Status* as an example, there's a good reason it is available in both print (V) and audio (A), and I also have Stadium Status coaching and training programs (K) built around the concepts in this book.

You

Your success and your ability to garner attention are about mindshare. In Troy's example with *Nashville Star*, the attention is helpful for him as the show host, but most of it is directed to the network. The networks and, often, the shows last longer in the consumer's mind than the host. This is why you need to amplify major appearances using other media. It keeps your story in the news and expands your reach. While it would be nice to be everywhere, you have to at least *appear* like you're everywhere. Want to get greater mindshare? You need at least seven points of reference for people to help them connect the dots about who you are and what you do. Recognize that you have options—you can go where the fish are in unique and creative ways.

The seven points of reference both for Cowboy Troy and for me all relate directly to the core value proposition we offer. A great way for you to make sure your sevens link back to your brand's central message is to place your points of reference in a Venn diagram.

A Venn diagram is a set of circles in which varying portions of each circle may overlap. Each circle would represent one of your points of reference. Your seven points of reference don't need to overlap completely or even significantly, just enough to help people connect the dots. Think of the areas of overlap as having doorways. The doors swing open on each circle and allow your prospects into your world. Once they are in, they may move from one circle to the next. (I have included a Venn diagram for you to use in the Stadium Steps at the end of this chapter.)

If all you did was create one method (think traditional sales funnel), there's only one doorway in. And when there's only one way in, you are limiting your ability to gain people's attention much less retain their attention. With seven points of reference you are creating seven attractive methods for people to find you and connect what you do with who you are.

Repetition is the key to success.

Repetition is the key to success.

Repetition is the key to success.

In your quest to create at least seven points of reference, you'll probably feel like your message is getting incredibly redundant. That's all in your head, not anyone else's. The fact is that, until you feel like a broken record, your message most likely isn't connecting the dots and getting through to your audience. Just like people need seven points of reference, they also need to hear your specific message, pitch, request, or call to action at least seven times before they will feel compelled to take action on it. Stay the course, and execute the plan beyond your own boredom—that's where the gold is.

Stadium Steps

1. Moving clockwise through the diagram, choose seven points of reference that will help people connect who you are with what you do. Keep in mind the VAK model, and make sure your seven points of reference are multimodal by incorporating all three learning styles.
2. Understanding the VAK learning model can be critical in relating to and coaching your clients and employees. Consider this: if all you did was talk to your team at work, and only one-third of your people are auditory learners, your message would have less of an impact on their professional development and growth than if you used additional methods as well. Consider asking your employees to take a VAK test; numerous versions are available online.

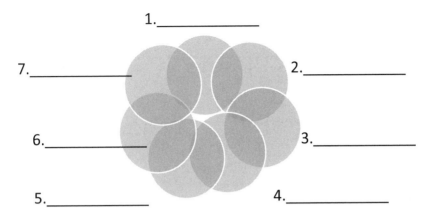

Figure 9.1 *VAK model/Venn diagram*

CHAPTER 10

Chase Excellence

Make sure your diamond is as polished as it can be.
—Sonny Throckmorton, country music singer

The most valuable business and life advice I ever received came from an unlikely source in an impromptu moment—in, of all places, a stadium. In 1994 Michael West, one of my best friends from college, was working for the New Jersey Nets when the franchise brought in football coaching icon Lou Holtz to speak to the organization. The employees were allowed to bring guests, and Mike was kind enough to invite me.

I was brand new to the coaching profession and, since I had a chance to meet with Coach Holtz after his talk, I asked him this question: "What is the best piece of advice you'd give someone new to the coaching profession?" Holtz responded, "It's the same advice I'd give anyone of any age in any profession. When people meet you they are asking themselves three things about you: Can I trust you? Do you care about me? Are you committed to excellence?"

He went on to explain that they are asking these things in priority order. If they can't trust you, the answers to questions two and three don't really matter. From that day forward, Holtz's three-question test has been my compass both personally and professionally. With that in mind, I need to flip the script on the chapter format and lead with examples from my personal experience, then give you the ultimate stadium status examples of the right way to chase excellence.

Bru

Two companies I'd been patronizing for quite some time have lost my business. Their failings serve as a cautionary tale for every entrepreneur on how to handle gaining and maintaining clients. One, an online marketing firm, began with a singular focus and was becoming an industry leader. It began experiencing systematic failures as a direct result of what is often referred to as mission creep. Essentially, the company didn't stay in its lane, and as a result a lack of focus caused it to repeatedly drop the ball. These are services I use in my business on a daily basis and will for the foreseeable future—I'll just be using one of its competitors now.

The other company was at one point a local business but tried to expand too fast, and shifted focus away from valuable existing customers like me (which would have resulted in endless referrals). Its focus went to geographic expansion in the hope that would produce growth. In the process, the company hired untrained or, at best, undertrained staff who could not problem solve, much less be proactive with clients.

In both cases, the businesses hit a point where they failed the three-question test. I could no longer trust them. Given their mission creep, I didn't feel they cared about me anymore, and by chasing money instead of quality they demonstrated that they were not committed to excellence.

The last example is that of a sporting goods company I did some short-term consulting work for. It struggled to gain market share and the reasons for its difficulties quickly became apparent. The company wasn't known for any one sport or piece of equipment, as it tried to be all things to all people. The consequence of that lack of focus was widespread breakage and quality control issues. Consequently, the sales reps didn't believe in the products and didn't use the products. The company even hired a spokesperson to endorse the product, but she would only be photographed with the equipment for ads and wouldn't actually use it in games. When I told company executives not to enter into that endorsement relationship and they ignored me, I fired them. They failed all three of the questions in Holtz's test. Without trust, there can be no care, and without both trust and care you can never be committed to excellence. Furthermore, there was no congruence; the sales reps didn't trust the quality of the product and neither did the spokesperson. If you're not confident about the quality, you can't effectively represent the brand.

As a result, it was no surprise that customers didn't trust the quality of the product either. People don't judge us by our words, they decide based on our actions. Those actions can have significant consequences in terms of lost business and damaged brand equity.

Them

The greatest shining example of the right way to build a stadium status business is the Marucci Baseball Bat Company, now known as Marucci Sports. The company began in 2002 in founder Jack Marucci's backyard wood shed in Baton Rouge, Louisiana. Marucci Sports is built on a solid commitment to an unparalleled level of consistency and craftsmanship. Instead of focusing on growth or diversification, it simply focused on excellence. Interestingly, growth and diversification are a natural byproduct of excellence.

The massive success of Marucci Sports is perhaps the most stadium status example of the three-question test. Those who run the company live their mission. Marucci has never paid a spokesperson; each professional athlete who represents and endorses Marucci bats is actually an investor in the company. They've made that physical, emotional, and financial commitment. A bat is to a baseball player what a scalpel is to a surgeon. In other words, precise tasks with high stakes require state-of-the-art equipment of the highest quality.

The company has become the standard of excellence in its industry. Because it has built trust, cares about its customers, and has a clear, ever-present commitment to excellence, Marucci is now able to diversify its offerings to include baseball gloves and helmets.

It's an organization that has never deviated from its focus, which is why I would argue that it has achieved best-in-class status in professional stadiums around the country. Marucci is to the baseball bat as Stradivarius is to the violin. To quote Jack Marucci, "Don't chase the dollar—chase excellence, and the dollars will take care of themselves."

Every Marucci bat is game-ready, and a little leaguer (think, smallest customer) receives the same quality bat as a major-league player (think, key account). That's a lesson on trust, care, and commitment to excellence every business can learn from. This simple yet powerful strategy of chasing excellence, not money, has made the company one of the top brands in baseball bats.

Ask yourself, do you buy what you're selling? In other words, how can anyone trust you if you don't practice what you preach?

In the fall of 2015, outdoor and fitness goods retail chain REI shocked the world by making a major announcement that it would be closing its stores on Black Friday. REI called it an #OptOutside initiative; I call it a stadium status move. In fact, it was the ultimate stadium status move, and you should do the same thing. I'm not talking about closing your store. What I'm referring to is believing so strongly in what you do that you actually live it. REI's #OptOutside initiative is a great example of being fearlessly unapologetic about living your mission. While some may believe that REI closing all seventy-six of its stores on Black Friday may be a lost revenue opportunity, I'm telling you that its fearlessly unapologetic and authentic stance will create new customers, cement more intense loyalty amongst existing customers, and just may spark a crusade to reel in some of the insanity that is Black Friday shopping.

A colleague once asked me an interesting question: What's the single greatest business development tool you have? My answer was much like REI's Black Friday move—it's practicing what I preach. I'm a coach, but every month I scratch a fairly sizable check to someone who coaches me.

You

Do you believe strongly enough in what you're selling that you buy it yourself? Do your people? If not, you're in bigger trouble than you think, because that means you're not emotionally and personally invested in the very thing you claim is valuable to the marketplace. Owning it yourself first, rather than simply trying to sell it to someone else, is the difference between lip service and putting your money where your mouth is. Your prospects can sense your investment. When you are invested, people see that you're making a physical, emotional, and financial commitment that is heartfelt. What you do and what you say are congruent.

Maybe, like me, you're not selling a physical product. You still need to be invested; otherwise, you will lose in the marketplace to those who are. When prospective clients tell me they are interviewing several coaches, I share with them the names of my coaches and encourage them to ask the other professionals they're interviewing who their coach is. If the coaches can't answer that question, they don't believe in what they sell enough to buy it themselves. Essentially, you would be entering a do-as-I-say-not-as-I-do relationship. Game over. I have yet to lose a prospective client based on my response, which tells you something about the incongruence in my profession. I bet yours isn't all that different. Do you believe in what you're selling enough to actually invest in it yourself first? If you're not willing to pay for it, how can you expect anyone else to value it? As the great American philosopher Sammy Kershaw once said: "If you ain't lived it, there ain't no use in singin' it."

I strongly encourage you to rethink your growth strategy, because we are all far better off staying in our respective lanes, so we can gain and maintain a level of excellence that engenders greater trust, demonstrates deep caring, and shows near flawless execution. Once you've become best in class and your competition is a distant second, then and only then is it time to diversify your offerings in related categories.

Think beyond the cautionary tales I shared with you from vendors I used, to some of the famous failures of brands that didn't stay in their lanes and created a lack of trust or loss of faith among their customers.

- Do you remember the McDonald's pizza? They probably hope you don't. McDonald's is famous for one thing: hamburgers. After all, it proudly boasts its "billions sold total" underneath the golden arches on every sign.
- How about the ESPN cell phone? Do you recall this short-lived, short-sighted lane change that the number-one brand among men probably wishes it hadn't attempted? After all, ESPN is known as the worldwide leader in sports news, not the worldwide leader in cellular communications.
- Ladies, do you remember Harley-Davidson perfume? Guys, how about Harley-Davidson aftershave? The motorcycle manufacturer has an iconic, global brand and a cult-like following, but diversifying beyond world-class motorcycles to products like perfume and aftershave simply wasn't congruent with the brand. It was too much of a stretch beyond the biker jackets, pants, and clothing that made sense for the brand. (I probably shouldn't even mention the short-lived Harley-Davidson wine coolers.)

The lesson from these cautionary tales is that more products doesn't necessarily mean more revenue or greater reach. Sometimes, overextending your
brand backfires and actually waters down your brand, because Holtz's three-
question test is constantly playing out in your customers' minds, whether you
realize it or not.

Stadium Steps

1. What is your number-one, hands-down, core offering? When someone
   says your brand's name, what do people immediately think of?
2. Based on your answer to #1, do you deliver that core offering better than
   anyone else?
3. How can you take the answer to #1 and improve upon that signature
   offering to make it shine even brighter (even if you're already operating
   at a world-class level)?
4. Incorporate the three-question test in every interaction, hiring decision,
   and new business development meeting with a prospective client or
   partner.

CHAPTER 11

Satisfaction Guaranteed

We're going to win Sunday. I guarantee it.
—Joe Namath, Hall of Fame NFL quarterback

Do you believe there is a stadium status leader and entrepreneur already inside you? I 100 percent guarantee you there is, but you may not have realized it yet. Here's the proof . . .

Count the number of F's in this sentence:

> FINISHED FILES ARE THE RESULT OF YEARS
> OF SCIENTIFIC STUDY COMBINED WITH THE
> EXPERIENCE OF MANY YEARS.

How many F's did you count?

The correct answer is six. If you're like most people who read that sentence, you counted three or four F's, maybe five. But I doubt you counted six. You didn't realize there were six F's, but they were all there the whole time.

You may not realize that you have what it takes to be a stadium status leader or entrepreneur, but I promise you that all the ability you need is already inside you. You just need to trust yourself and unleash it. When you have the courage to let your talents loose and offer a no-questions-asked, 100 percent satisfaction guarantee, that confidence will be contagious—others will see it, feel it, and feed off it.

The value of a guarantee isn't in the "price tag" of what you have to offer, it's an intangible. A guarantee demonstrates two things to your audience: (1) your confidence in your ability to deliver the goods and (2) the quality of the product.

When you offer a personal guarantee of what you do, you can more confidently command the fee your product or your service is worth. Why? Because low pricing is the last resort of those who don't have an exceptional product or service and can't figure out how to overdeliver value.

When your offering is cutting edge, trustworthy, reliable, and high quality, people won't view your fee as an expense as much as they will see it as an investment.

Them

Tom Osborne, athletic director and retired football coach at the University of Nebraska, was convinced by entrepreneur and regional FieldTurf distributor Jim Gerking to hop on a Learjet and fly to a Cumberland, Maryland, high school stadium to meet John Gilman of FieldTurf Inc., to inspect a new type of artificial turf called FieldTurf, which contained crushed rubber. (Nebraska was looking to replace the AstroTurf surface on Memorial Field at the time.)

When Osborne arrived he asked Gilman, "So where's this artificial turf field you want me to look at?" Gilman replied, "You just walked across it, Coach!" The artificial turf looked and felt so real that Osborne was sold on the spot.

Osborne was so impressed with the product that he became an investor and consultant for FieldTurf. Later that year, Osborne and Gerking pitched Field-Turf to Lincoln Public Schools for their stadium. Because the product was new and the two of them had never done an installation, school board members asked, "What if it falls apart?" Osborne piped up, "I'll personally guarantee it. If it falls apart within eight years I'll replace it out of my pocket." They were sold on the spot.

Nebraska was the first division one football team to play on FieldTurf, and after that installation in 1999 sales went through the roof. Thousands of athletic fields are now made of FieldTurf.

An empire was started by one man making a personal guarantee.

Bru

If you go to my website you'll find my guarantee in the form of a "100% Money Back Guarantee" emblem on every page involving a potential customer transaction. For example, my speaking, coaching, and consulting pages all contain it. Click the emblem, and you arrive at my guarantee page, www.coachbru.com/satisfaction-guarantee/, which contains the following details.

Coaching & Consulting

I stand behind and assure you of the quality of my work with this guarantee.

If you find that the objectives for the project are not being met according to the measures of success that we have agreed upon, I will continue to work on the project at no additional fee beyond expense reimbursement until we concur that the objectives are met.

Failing that, I will refund all fees paid.

Store Purchases

Order Today With Confidence.

Complete your order today and if for any reason you don't absolutely love this product within the next 90 days, we'll refund you NO QUESTIONS ASKED.

It's as simple as calling our customer service department at 207.576.9853 or sending us a refund request email to john@coachbru.com.

You read that correctly—I offer a 100 percent money-back guarantee for any reason. For that matter, if you find this book doesn't meet or exceed your expectations, e-mail or call me personally and I will refund your money, no questions asked. I also don't do contracts with clients; if a client wants to cancel ongoing work with me at any time, he is free to do so. The last thing I want is someone to feel locked into an arrangement. If I can't deliver the results, I believe my clients should have the flexibility and freedom to move on. I am that confident in my programs and my ability to deliver results for clients. My track record reflects it in the form of positive reviews, testimonials, and feedback.

After ten years in business, thousands of books and information products sold, hundreds of speaking engagements and consulting and coaching clients, I have yet to receive a complaint much less a request for a refund on any product or service I've delivered. This is the beauty of the personal guarantee: you put clients at ease and remove any pressure or fear of buyer's remorse from their minds. It takes a powerful objection off the table before it becomes one.

Osborne could have led his FieldTurf sales pitch with the guarantee rather than allowing the school board to bring up the question, "What if it falls apart?"

Confidence is contagious. How confident are you in your ability to deliver results? Are you buying what you're selling?

The real estate market where I live is incredibly competitive and highly saturated with Realtors. There are more than 4000 agents in a state so small that it's ranked forty-first nationally in population size. But there's one agent who is so uniquely differentiated she is a category of one. Her name is Kathy Manchester, and her competitive advantage is a simple personal guarantee you will find in all her marketing and advertising: "If I can't sell your house for you, I'll buy it from you."

Who would you list your house with, the agent who hopes to sell it for you or the one who guarantees that if she can't sell it, she'll buy it from you? That's a stadium status move if I ever saw one. Manchester is smart enough to know that she'll sell clients on her services if she can remove their biggest objection before it even comes up.

You

The most valuable real estate you can own is the six inches between your ears, in the form of a confident mindset. When you put your money where your mouth is, you show up as more confident, and that confidence is contagious.

Providing a guarantee to your clients is incredibly important for two reasons.

1. The prospect does not really know exactly what he or she is buying. This is especially true when you're selling a service or an intangible.
2. The odds are good that your prospect may have come to you as a result of a bad experience with another company or service provider in your industry. By offering a personal guarantee, you're removing the risk from them and placing it squarely on your shoulders.

If you really believe in the value you offer, this should all be easy. If you can't personally guarantee your offer, you really need to go back to the drawing board and create better products and services.

- How will you personally guarantee that your product will stand the test of time? Will you replace it out of pocket like Tom Osborne did?
- Are you willing to take a page out of my playbook and offer a money-back guarantee for your services or the experience you provide your audience?
- If you operate in real estate or any type of consignment sales, would you be bold enough to offer to buy the item yourself from a client if you can't sell it for them?

Stadium Steps

1. Commit to executing a 100 percent, no-questions asked, money-back guarantee. (You'll thank me later.)
2. Learn what creates the most sales reluctance for your audience and craft a guarantee that addresses that issue.
3. Give your clients a bold, strong, and lengthy guarantee. Don't offer a two-week or thirty-day guarantee—offer a longer one. Short guarantees make the prospect feel pressure to make a decision. A guarantee of at least a couple of months reduces time pressure. Give them a year or a lifetime guarantee, and you've completely eliminated the time pressure for them. The longer the refund, the more trust it engenders. Hyundai differentiated itself and built its business by boldly offering a ten-year, 100,000-mile powertrain warrantee. Talk about bold, strong, and long!
4. Include your guarantee in your advertising and marketing collateral. Domino's Pizza built its brand on its ads in the 1980s: "Hot pizza delivered in thirty minutes or it's free." The ads have ended and the guarantee has changed but people still remember and talk about that promise.
5. Create a seal, and display it prominently with your guarantee on your website and in your office or retail space.
6. Don't make your clients fill out a form. Make it easy for your audience to invoke the guarantee in the rare event someone wants a refund.

CHAPTER 12

Put Your Fans on Speed Dial

Country music busts the wall between performer and audience.
There's a connection because there's a vulnerability.
—Hunter Hayes, American singer and songwriter

They say truth is stranger than fiction. I would add that the science fiction of just a few years ago has become nonfiction today. The most powerful business resource entrepreneurs possess resides right in their pockets and the pockets of their audience. It's your smartphone, and it's capable of much more than what was predicted by *Star Trek* and *The Jetsons* combined. You have the ability to reach virtually anyone on the planet at any time in multiple ways and in real time. Whether it's a live two-way video conference, live-streaming video, or simply messages shared via text, audio, or video across a variety of platforms, your smartphone can connect you to potential clients and new audiences at the push of a button—in most cases, for free.

You don't need a massive advertising budget or an expensive public relations campaign, and you aren't reliant on mainstream media to create attention for your brand. You can reach your customers and prospects directly. And if you're smart, you'll encourage them to reach out to you directly as well. There has never been a better time or a bigger opportunity for you to grow your audience than there is now. The question is, are you bold enough to do it?

What can an entrepreneur learn from a college football coach? A lot. Coaches are a lot like entrepreneurs; they're in the business of talent acquisition, their performance is measured on a scoreboard every quarter, and just like you, their job security is contingent on their ability to deliver great results. Coaching and entrepreneurship are the same as other industries in that there's the 1 percent who are changing the game and then there's the other 99 percent who are just staying the same.

Them

I'd like to introduce you to two innovators whose workplaces are, literally, stadiums. Both the music business and collegiate sports are copycat industries:

most people will copy what they see successful peers doing in the hope of achieving similar results. Sadly, imitation and duplication will always leave you a step behind and label you as one of many rather than one of a kind. Blake Anderson and John King are two industry giants who have elevated and separated themselves from the competition by blazing their own trail rather than following the herd. And that herd mentality isn't limited to college football and the music industry—it's alive and well in all our professions. Anderson and King, however, are living proof of the power of personal connection in building a stadium status brand.

Meet Blake Anderson

Blake Anderson, the most entrepreneurial coach in America, is one of the game changers in his industry. He's the architect of the most creative football program in the United States, the Arkansas State Red Wolves. He's one of the few in his profession who is keenly aware that the game has changed, so to speak. College sports, like business, has entered an era in which getting great results isn't who you know or what you know, it's who knows you. And to get known you've got to be different, or you'll be invisible.

At a program like Arkansas State, which is located in a small town and doesn't have the benefit of being the state's flagship university or having membership in a major conference, great results are contingent on the ability to market better, faster, and with fewer resources. How do you beat the big dogs at their own game when you're a smaller brand, are operating in a smaller market, or have a smaller budget? Not by doing the same things the other programs are doing, but by changing the game.

Whether you call it a disruptive strategy or guerilla marketing, creativity is the foundation of Arkansas State's strategy for building a winner. Anderson asks his staff the same question each day: What is no one else doing right now that we can pull off? You should be asking yourself and your team that same daily question.

Anderson says of his philosophy, "Whatever I do I'm going to get media attention for our program," and, boy, does he ever. Success leaves clues, and the following examples are a compilation of "greatest hits" that Anderson has produced. You should try to pull off your own version of them.

1. *Trick plays*. ASU regularly runs trick plays. The players have fun with them, the plays are hard for the competition to prepare for, and they entertain fans. In fact, the plays are so popular that #ArkansasState was trending on Twitter during a Florida versus Florida State game on a Saturday night (while neither of those teams were). Arkansas State had played earlier in the day and had run a trick play that captured the national media spotlight and went viral with more than ten million YouTube views.

2. *eBay auctions*. For the past two years, Anderson has auctioned off a stint as guest coach of the spring game on eBay, and each time an entrepreneur

has won the bid. The move was so unique that it made national news, and the NCAA subsequently investigated its legality and found nothing wrong. In addition to becoming a new revenue stream, the strategy created new fans for life and has become an ASU tradition.

3. *"Traffic tickets."* The day before the homecoming game, Anderson handed out game tickets to folks sitting in traffic. Wearing a GoPro camera on his head, Anderson filmed the entire event for promotional purposes, and the video was picked up by national media outlets like *Sports Illustrated.*

Lots of businesses want to grow new fans but flounder because they use traditional means of business development, which have a very limited ROI; by following the herd and utilizing the same strategies that every other business in the industry uses, they've essentially been blocked from the minds of the consumers they're trying to reach. If you've ever fast-forwarded your DVR through a commercial you know exactly what I'm talking about. The way to move from out of mind to top of mind is to stand out. For example, a local cellular provider in my hometown frequently runs a tab for a couple hours for Starbucks customers in its local market: no selling, no advertising, just surprising and delighting folks. Consider giving out free samples, letting prospects test-drive your service, or granting temporary use of your product. Give your prospective customers a reason to come back.

4. *Ice cream for the student section on game day.* Those in the student section are ASU's most rabid fans, and offering them a treat is a surefire attention grabber. What can you do to surprise and delight your fans? Create a VIP client appreciation event or provide them with a special bonus.

Crazy? Yes. Different? Yes. Off the wall? Yes. But the bottom line is, these gambits work. The tangible benefit of Blake Anderson's "different" strategy: ticket sales, revenue, donations, and attendance are all up at Arkansas State as a result of his culture of creativity.

Here's why Anderson's tricks work: people pay attention because they wonder what Anderson is going to do next. You want to leave your audience wanting more as well. Human beings love little unexpected moments and experiences. The emotions that result from these positive moments make the experience memorable and make us want to share the story with others. Our brains are actually hardwired to derive pleasure from unexpected surprises.

Meet John King

John King is to country music what Coach Anderson is to college football. They're definitely kindred spirits and share the same philosophy that I do: be different or be invisible.

When King gave out his cell phone number during his concert at the 2015 Old Port Festival, I thought he was crazy. I watched almost every girl in the crowd plug his number into her phone, and I told my daughter Meredith to type his number into her phone and text him that we enjoyed his show. Within twenty minutes of stepping off the stage he responded, and she showed me his text thanking her for coming to the show.

Then I realized he's not crazy, he's crazy like a fox. That night I texted John King and asked to schedule an interview, and he responded almost instantly. King's goal is to build a personal connection with his fans, one to one, and at deeper level than most artists.

The genesis of his phone number strategy goes back to his philosophy on marketing his brand. When he was a new artist he realized he had to do things differently. His whole philosophy is centered on one question he asked his staff: "What's something John King can do that no one else does?" That something became giving out his cell phone number.

In this day and age everyone has a cell phone, and King found a unique way to use the technology to his advantage. For the past year King has been giving out his cell phone number at concerts, and it's taken his brand to a new stratosphere.

While King's gesture is not about the money, he's certainly not going to leave money on the table by not saving your cell phone number. King responds to every single text personally, and after each tour stop he exports the fan contact information into a database labeled by city and then uses it to message his fans the next time he is scheduled to perform in their area. King is an entertainer but he also understands that he is the CEO of John King, Incorporated. He's the brand, and he knows that, while his record label, publicists, and promoters all work to market his brand, none of them is going to care as much or work as hard for John King as John King will. I might add that King is the king at connection. It's no small coincidence that he was a marketing major and minored in music business at the University of Georgia. That undergraduate degree in marketing sure has come in handy.

The level of access and personal attention King gives is not only uncommon, it's incomparable. The best of the best are connectors. They understand that, whatever profession they're in, they are in the relationship business first.

Stadium Status, Literally

Mark Cuban, owner of the Dallas Mavericks NBA franchise, puts his personal e-mail address on the Jumbotron and asks fans for feedback and suggestions on how to improve the in-stadium experience. Instead of sitting in the owner's luxury suite, as virtually all other sports team owners do, he sits courtside, next to the fans, and connects with them. It's something he does that no one else in his position does. This practice has transformed Cuban's business and cemented his fans' loyalty. Here's one point of proof that Cuban listens to and acts on fan feedback: he had a shot clock with more than one face manufactured for the arena so that fans could see how much time was left on the clock wherever they were sitting. This improvement was based on an e-mail from a fan who told him that from some seats in the arena it wasn't possible to read the clock.

When was the last time you called on a music star, a CEO, or one of the most universally respected coaches in America and were able to gain access, with no gatekeeper and no e-mail autoresponder?

Bru

By simply texting BRU to 22828 you can subscribe to my e-newsletter, and when you do so, you automatically receive a free e-book. It's not merely a gift or a way for me to add people to my mailing list. For me, it's the continuation of a relationship with many readers and the start of a relationship with other readers as well as coaching and speaking clients. My newsletter isn't written or sent by anyone other than yours truly each week, unless I invite a guest contributor to share an article. The e-mail address the newsletter originates from isn't some nonresponsive account or service, it's my personal e-mail address. If you want to hit reply and send me feedback, ask a question, or say hello, you will get me. The same goes for the phone number on my website. It doesn't automatically go to a voicemail system or my assistant, it rings in my pocket. Very few of my peers do this. I view it as a competitive advantage; you have direct access and don't have to sift through layers to get information to me. If you share your birthday with me you can count on receiving a birthday card on that day.

Don't simply be in the name accumulation business and try to add people to your list; instead, add so much value that they want to connect with you. Whether the connection is via text, e-mail, social media, or in person, it doesn't matter how you create value for your customers as long as you show that you care. Remember, you don't need to give people more ways to connect with you, you need to give them more reasons—ROR (return on relationship) trumps ROI (return on investment).

You may not be a music star or billionaire team owner but stadium status growth is simply a matter of building your audience one fan at a time. Is this level of personal connection a huge investment of time? Absolutely. Responding to tons of texts, in King's case, or e-mails, in my case or Cuban's, is a big commitment but it pays dividends.

Business building is about relationship building, and relationship building is about building a one-to-one connection. That level of personal attention and care takes the relationship to a whole new level, and leaves a positive impression so that people won't forget you. Isn't that your goal? It certainly is what your customer wants. People remember that you took the time to interact with them and respond to them. Why? Because it's uncommon. A lack of accessibility, responsiveness, and follow through are the norm today. Be uncommon. Be like John King and Mark Cuban—or like strength coach Ken Mannie.

When I spoke on career advancement at the 2015 national convention of the Collegiate Strength and Conditioning Coaches Association, I used Ken

Mannie, long-time strength coach at Michigan State Football, as an example of a person who built a stadium status brand in the field of strength and conditioning. He is an incomparable expert and a rock star in this profession. I shared with the coaches at the convention that Mannie became the foremost authority in the industry through personal connection and individual attention.

Shortly after the conference, Mannie called to thank me, not for mentioning him, but for the fact that my speech was exactly what the strength-training profession needed to hear. In an audience full of thousands of coaches, his was the only response I received. I was blown away. The closest comparison for you as an entrepreneur would be if Warren Buffett called you to say you give great financial advice. I responded right away with a handwritten note and sent copies of my books as a thank-you. Not just for his thoughtful call but for his help many years ago.

On our call, I asked him if he remembered a young coach writing to him in 1997 in response to an article he'd written about making a one-man wooden conditioning sled. He said that of the thousands of people who read the article he only got one response. I reminded him that respondent was me, and told him how impressed I was that he'd responded right away with a blueprint, a parts list, and a handwritten note. He remembered my letter and our ongoing conversation from back then and sent me a thoughtful gift of some Michigan State apparel and a very kind handwritten note.

The Lesson

Most people are too busy to notice or care about the little things. What separates stadium status professionals is that they realize that everything matters and the little things are really big things. These little things include connection, follow through, and a personal touch.

I never imagined in 1997 that the foremost expert in the field of strength and conditioning would bother to respond to a nobody like me, a first year coach at a small college. I've carried the life lesson Mannie taught me back then throughout my career, and I hope you carry it with you now. Be who you say you are. Answer your own e-mails and phone calls. You can't outsource personal attention and connection. Nothing says a company doesn't appreciate your call quite like a voice prompt telling you, "We appreciate your call; please hold for the next attendant."

The Lesson within the Lesson

We each affect a lot of people but often receive very little response or thanks. Focus on those who do respond. A lack of response doesn't mean apathy or disinterest; sometimes, as in the case of my talk, it's because you hit them right between the eyes with a reality that was helpful yet outside their comfort zone. Keep serving.

You

Though John King is in the music business, Mark Cuban is in the entertainment business, Ken Mannie is in the coaching business, and I am in the writing business, we are all in the relationship business. You are, too, and the best way to build a relationship is to connect, one fan at a time. King gives out his cell number, Cuban broadcasts his e-mail, and I utilize a text opt-in when I speak to associations and organizations. What is one thing you can do that no one else does?

Why you should invest in personal connection:

1. Trust in brands and government is at an all-time low. Therefore, we must behave differently. Enough said.
2. Change the conversation. People take to social media to share their emotions—look no further than TripAdvisor and Yelp reviews, many of which are venting and complaining about bad customer experiences. Spreading unexpected goodwill is like taking out an insurance policy to make the conversation about your brand a positive one.

When you take a chance you risk embarrassment, but if you're playing not to embarrass yourself you're not going to be noticed. If you want to be noticed, you have to be willing to take chances. People only pay attention when there's a sense of mystery.

The Empire Strikes Back is the most critically acclaimed *Star Wars* movie, in large part because the viewer is left with a sense of incompleteness at the end. Whether the subject is an iconic movie, ASU football, or your business, by defying expectations and adding an element of surprise people will keep tuning in because they will always be wondering, "I wonder what's going to happen next?"

If there's one thing I've learned in my career, it's that the best of the best are connectors. It's what elevates them to stadium status in their industry. They understand that direct lines of communication with their audience create and cement loyalty, which in turn cultivates passionate advocacy by the consumer for their brand.

Creativity, accessibility, and responsiveness are competitive advantages for stadium status businesses, and these same competitive advantages are available to you. The question is this: Are you willing to invest in innovating and executing? The following stadium steps will challenge you to build your competitive advantage. Remember the old saying, "No deposit, no return"? That doesn't just apply to bottles.

Stadium Steps

1. What is one thing you can do that no one else in your industry is doing?
2. How will you commit to being more responsive to your audience?

3. What can you execute—like Coach Anderson's trick plays—that's totally outside the box in your market to generate media attention? Remember: it's not who you know but who knows you.

4. What experiences can you give your customers that they wouldn't normally have access to? (Examples: interview a fan for your blog or podcast, raffle off chances to be boss for a day, give behind the scenes tours of your manufacturing facilities.)

CHAPTER 13

Your Tour Bus

The bus is probably the most important instrument in country music.
—Barbara Mandrell, American country singer and actress

Athletes and entertainers are acutely aware of travel and its impact, as they spend so much of their time on the road between performances. Time on the road can easily take a toll on performance if they're not very careful about how they travel. Some of the most valuable equipment in terms of facilitating great work is the mode of transportation. Take it from a road warrior, travel can make or break you. Literally.

When you schedule your listening tour I strongly encourage you to incorporate the travel strategy I'm about to share with you. Your time is the most valuable asset you possess, and it's a depreciating asset. You're either wasting, spending, or investing your time. Only when you're investing your time is it possible to get a return on that time. Sadly, so many people waste time when traveling. I know because I was guilty of it myself.

Whether you have a roster of fifty athletes or a dozen band members—and the tons of equipment that accompany either—the standard method of transportation is a bus. Charter buses for the teams and tour buses for the musicians.

Them

Bands perform well into the night, leave it all on the stage, and board the tour bus after the show, traveling through the night to the next destination.

When I interviewed Joe Shipley of Bull Shipley Touring Inc., he shared with me the biggest benefits artists derive from tour bus travel. It affords them an opportunity to rest, practice their craft, relax before a show, and, most importantly, arrive at their destination safe and well rested. The driver's job isn't simply to drive the bus, Shipley explained. It's to take the responsibility, stress, and headaches of travel logistics off the performer's plate.

The bus serves as a bedroom, office, and even a studio, where the artists can write songs, sing, and practice in a distraction-free environment. The bus provides an amazing creative space and home away from home for artists. They are able to operate in a productive, creative mindset because they feel safe and well rested.

Shipley currently drives for Granger Smith and his band. In 2015, the band performed 163 shows in eleven months. This put them on the road for 256 days, 93 of which were travel days, which means they essentially spent more than three months of their work year traveling. Imagine the lost productive time if the performers had to drive, navigate, and service the vehicle themselves. Instead, Smith and his crew have virtually every amenity you'd find at a traditional office suite, and then some. The jump seat (passenger seat) at the front of the bus serves as a private area and can be used to make business calls and give radio interviews. The front lounge is a social area and, given its layout, it serves much like a living room. The band can gather there to eat, drink, relax, watch television, or discuss work. The bunk area behind the front lounge serves as a bedroom and a place to take catnaps. There is also a rear lounge, which the tour manager can use as an office. A bathroom and shower on board allows them to avoid frequent or lengthy stops on the way to their destination.

Bru

I found in my work that when I hired a driver, I enjoyed the same freedom, relaxation, productivity, and other benefits Shipley's passengers experienced. During my coaching years, I had noticed a pattern with regard to my productivity. I was much more productive during the season (when, in theory, I should have been busier and more exhausted) and was significantly less productive in the summer, during recruiting season.

For a while I couldn't put my finger on exactly why this was true, but at the season's end I realized how much work I was able to get done while I was on the bus traveling to and from away games. Our season began in January and ended in May—seventeen-plus games a season over the course of five months. That provided a lot of time to get work done on the road, distraction free. Once summer recruitment travel began, I was driving rental cars for long hours, going from showcase to showcase. I'd arrive tired and rundown, spend the day in the hot sun recruiting, and crawl back to the hotel exhausted, only to wake up and do the same thing all over again. Imagine three straight months of that: 100 nights in hotel rooms and countless hours of driving. There's a lot of lost productive time when you have to keep a schedule like that. The rare occasions that I was able to fly to an event offered a welcome reprieve from the usual grind.

Early in my career as a professional speaker and author, I found the travel exhausting as well. Mainly because I was the one driving, navigating, fighting traffic, fueling up the vehicle, and searching for parking.

In 2014 I spoke at two international conferences in the United States, one in Vermont and one in Boston. I drove myself to the Vermont event, getting up before dawn in order to make it to the conference the same day I had to give my speech. I was navigating unfamiliar back roads, trying to find my way around detours (pretty much all roads in Northern New England are under construction in the springtime) and, as a result, I lost a workday. And I couldn't do any last-minute preparation or rehearsal. My presentation was in the evening, which made for a long day.

Two weeks later, for the Boston event, I hired a college student I knew to drive me to and from the event. I was able to answer phone calls, catch up on client e-mails, and make some last-minute adjustments to my presentation. No surprise, when I went back and reviewed the video from both events the results were very different. In Vermont I appeared low energy, looked tired, and didn't deliver a presentation that was up to my standards. Whether the audience knew it or not didn't matter; I knew it. Contrast this with the presentation I gave in Boston; it was essentially the same speech, but I was energetic, looked refreshed, and delivered one of my best performances.

Lesson learned. From that point forward, whenever possible, I adjust my method of travel to eliminate variables. In fact, my wife and I made the decision to move our family to a community closer to the airport. It's amazing how much better the quality of my work is when I take a flight or hire a driver.

Musician, college coach, and professional speaker are about the most unglamorous glamorous professions you'll find if you peek behind the scenes at "a day in the life." The one necessity that many view as a luxury is a comfortable method of travel—and there's no reason anyone in any industry can't travel the same way for their jobs.

You

When you have a big sales presentation, have to address the board of directors, or are meeting with potential investors, shouldn't you make sure you're well rested, clear-minded, relaxed, and prepared?

Athletes and entertainers realize they are the instrument and they need to keep the instrument finely tuned and well cared for in order to perform at an optimal level. If you don't engage in self-care heading into work with a client, your effectiveness will suffer. Like an athlete competing or an entertainer engaging an audience, you need to show up clear-minded, physically refreshed, and focused. A strenuous commute will leave you distracted, stressed out, and fatigued before you step on your stage to compete.

Time is your most valuable and depreciating asset. To look carefully at the value of your time, consider this: today is 20 percent of your workweek. Two workdays are 10 percent of your month. There are about twenty-one workdays in each month. If you lose two workdays each month to poor time management, laziness, or illness you lose more than a full month of workdays each year. If that doesn't scare you, I don't know what will. I'm not sure there's a more compelling reason to embrace the value of a single workday. Every day.

Your options depend on your finances and the resources at your disposal. Maybe a tour bus isn't in your budget, but with personal driver services like BeMyDD (bemyDD.com) and WeDriveU (wedriveU.com) as well as Uber, Lyft, and local limousine companies, there is no reason not to invest in travel that allows you to maximize your most valuable resources: your time and energy.

Before I was coaching at the stadium status level, back when I had a non-scholarship team at a small college with an even smaller travel budget, I made it a priority to find funds so the team could travel well and eat well. Usually, we had to raise the money ourselves, but it was well worth fundraising to provide our team with every resource possible to put them in a situation to be successful on game day. Ever watched a sporting event on television and hear the announcers comment that a team has "bus legs"? The expression *bus legs* means the team looks slow or lethargic on the field. It's usually because they traveled to the game on the day of the game rather than arriving the night before and getting a good night's rest. Trust me, putting fifteen players who average about six feet tall and 200 pounds into a cramped van early in the morning on the day of a game is a recipe for failure. The coaches are physically and mentally fatigued from all that driving before they even step out on the field to start their actual workday. Never mind the fact that they have to drive the vans home afterward when, especially after a loss, they are mentally preoccupied, physically exhausted, and potentially in a bad mood.

I mention this scenario to you as a cautionary tale to get you to stop and reflect on just how often you do the exact same thing I just described. In an effort to pinch pennies, you leave for an event on the day it's planned, you drive yourself, and after your event you immediately hustle back home. The same goes for not eating well on the road. Just like a high-performance sports car, your engine needs rest, maintenance, and quality fuel in order to function at a high level.

At what level do you value yourself, your health, and your wealth? If you're traveling the day of the event, doing the driving yourself, eating on the cheap, and returning late into the night all in the name of saving money, guess what? It's probably actually costing you money. The cost is in the fact that you've made the mistake of not giving yourself or your employees (if they're the ones doing the traveling) every resource possible to put yourselves in the best position to be successful. Trust me, like the television announcers who can spot road-weary teams playing with bus legs, your prospects and clients can tell when you're performing at less than your best. It leaves a lasting and unflattering mark.

Let's do something about it now.

Stadium Steps

1. Look back over the last year on your calendar. Calculate the number of days you spent traveling.

2. How many workdays did you lose?

3. How much lost revenue do those missed workdays represent?

4. How many Saturdays or Sundays did you lose that you could've spent with your loved ones or could've invested in some renewal and recovery?

5. Looking at your schedule for the next six months, what opportunities exist to either upgrade or switch your mode of transportation to make you the passenger rather than the driver? For how many of those dates can you leave the day before your event?

6. Delegate your travel. Hire a travel agent or administrative assistant who can book your travel and contract to have you transported privately. Does your area have Uber? BeMyDD? WeDriveU?

7. If none of the private car services referenced in #6 exists in your community or state, I guarantee you there's a hungry college student or intern available. They work cheap and will be happy to make a little extra pocket cash transporting you around. (Bru Tip: Feed them well and they'll be eternally grateful, as they tend to exist on cheap beer, ramen noodles, and cafeteria food.)

CHAPTER 14

Shock and Awe

Surprise is the greatest gift which life can grant us.
—Boris Pasternak, novelist

Shock and awe is a term that was popularized during the George W. Bush administration in reference to air strikes on Iraq. In the military, it means using overwhelming power and amazing displays of force to paralyze the enemy's perception of the battlefield and destroy its will to fight. After the US invasion of Iraq in 2003, the expression became common business lingo, and it has been used ever since in reference to marketing.

In the military, the concept is also known as rapid dominance, and that is the perfect term for it in the business context as well. Essentially, brands look to make a dramatic display and create a strong first impression so they can eclipse the competition. The strategy involves instant, massive levels of action intended to influence the target audience. The more you can operate with surgical precision to establish a robust presence, the more effective the perception of your dominance will be.

As the saying goes, "You never get a second chance to make a first impression."

Them

What do a halftime show and a hamburger have in common? A lot, as it turns out. Many people may view these two things as being fairly pedestrian. At most establishments, a hamburger is just a round slab of beef on a bun. There's nothing terribly remarkable about a hamburger—unless you're Slater's 50/50 burger. A halftime show at a sporting event tends to be fairly run-of-the-mill entertainment. It's not the main attraction, it's an intermission from the main attraction—unless you're Big & Rich.

I'd like to introduce you to two examples of showmanship and differentiation that will serve as compelling examples of why you should incorporate shock and awe into your brand offering. The country music duo Big & Rich and restaurateur Scott Slater demonstrate how shock and awe can be a high-impact solution that radically transforms the way you differentiate and deliver your product or service.

Meet Big & Rich

In 2005, at halftime of the NBA All-Star Game, the halftime show performers made their entrance onto the court . . . on horseback, accompanied by cheer-leaders. The duo was Big & Rich, and they proceeded to shock and awe the audience with their hit song "Save a Horse, Ride a Cowboy." Cowboy Troy was touring with them, and he recalls seeing Jay Z, Beyoncé, and P-Diddy Combs in the front row absolutely captivated by what they were witnessing. Three hip hop artists among a crowd of thousands were blown away by the performance. It takes a lot to impress your peers, especially peers in another genre, one that typically doesn't share much of a crossover audience. I remember watching the commentators discussing the duo's entrance even as the game went into the second half. For the two musicians, the shock and awe of their entrance was mission accomplished, again.

Unbeknownst to most of that NBA crowd, this wasn't the first time the duo pulled such a shock and awe–filled entrance. A year earlier, at the 2004 ACM awards, Big & Rich were invited to walk the red carpet. They decided to tweak that "walk" just a little bit. Their red carpet entrance became a re-creation of their "Save a Horse" music video, which had been shot on the Shelby Street pedestrian bridge in Nashville. The duo entered on horseback, followed by the cast of characters in the video, which included a marching band, cheerlead-ers, a group of women in dominatrix costumes, Two-Foot Fred (a dwarf), and members of their Muzik Mafia collaborative dressed as mob bosses.

The entrance was pure, unadulterated shock and awe. They immediately stole the show, as their appearance created such massive attention that it became all anyone spoke about during and after the event. Their appearance upstaged everyone and everything else at the game. Mission accomplished.

Meet Slater's 50/50 Burger

Scott Slater founded Slater's 50/50 Burgers of California out of his love of beers, burgers, and bacon. The first time I walked into one of the restaurants while visiting San Diego, I remember thinking the entire place was a study in shock and awe. Everything is over the top. They have more than a hundred beers on tap and a trademarked name for the signature menu item, the 50/50 burger, which is 50 percent ground beef and 50 percent ground bacon.

I was so blown away by the first impression, the vibe in the restaurant, and the experience I had to interview the founder, Scott Slater. His first comment during our interview was, "Good, I'm glad you were blown away. We want guests to say, 'I can't believe these guys are doing this.'" Slater described the first impression they strive for by saying, "Visual stimulation is our goal. From serving 40 ounce beers in paper bags to boasting a burger that has a record-setting highest calorie count, we don't shy away from attention or sugar coat anything."

If simple shock and awe weren't enough, Slater's coined the term "Excesstasy," which Scott Slater defines as "the overwhelming feeling of excitement when indulging in new Slater's 50/50 menu items."

I felt an obligation to try the Peanut Butter & Jellousy burger, which consists of 100 percent Black Canyon Angus beef, thick-cut bacon, peanut butter, and strawberry jelly on a honey wheat bun. (I recommend having it a la mode, with a scoop of vanilla ice cream on top.) The restaurant keeps the shock and awe of Slater's from getting old by having customers design burgers and featuring them on their website, social media, and advertisements. It creates shock and awe all over again each time a new one is posted.

There are a lot of places you can get a hamburger, but there's only one 50/50 burger, and by allowing guests to design their own burger Slater's allows them to take emotional ownership of the restaurant, which is a lesson for every business owner. Slater commented that if it were normal it wouldn't be fun, and his philosophy is, if you're not having fun, you're doing it wrong.

Bru

In my past career as a radio show host and sales manager, I employed shock-and-awe marketing to grow our advertising and sponsorship revenue. The shock-and-awe marketing that elevated and separated my radio station from others in the market was smaller in scale than Big & Rich's halftime arrival on horseback, but it was equal in financial impact for our brand. I was new to the radio industry and to my position, but I made up for my lack of experience with creativity and hustle. I created my own shock-and-awe marketing campaign.

I would identify the top advertising and sponsorship prospects in our market and would mail them a shoe box. The box would be sent registered mail so the decision maker had to sign for it and the package would not be opened by a gatekeeper who would dismiss it or relegate it to the junk mail pile. Occasionally, I would even have a member of the station's promotional team or an intern deliver the package in person.

The box was professionally wrapped, so it looked almost as nice as a wedding gift. Inside the shoe box the prospect would find a plastic foot. It was wrapped in tissue paper, just like a pair of shoes would normally be wrapped in a shoe box. Attached to the big toe of the plastic foot was a "toe tag." It was really a handwritten note from me, with an invitation explaining,

> Now that I have a foot in the door, I'd like to invite you to be a special guest on my sports talk show. It can help drive more customers' feet through your doors. Enclosed is a CD of our show and samples of our

creative commercial production. I will call you on ABC date at XYZ time to schedule your interview.

Eight or nine times out of ten, I never had a chance to make that phone call because the business owners or CEOs would pick up the phone and call me to schedule a meeting immediately after receiving their shock-and-awe package. More than 75 percent of the time I won their business at that first meeting. On occasion, I was told that they decided to go with us because if our station could market their business on air half as well as I marketed myself, the decision was a no-brainer.

The cost of this promotion:

- Squeaky foot dog toy, $5.00
- Shoe box: FREE
- Toe tag card: FREE
- Gift wrap and tissue paper: $1.79
- Postage: $4.25
  Total: $11.04

The return on my eleven bucks was consistently in the thousands of dollars. Money well spent? Absolutely, and it sure as heck beat cold calling. Occasionally, the maneuver would rub the recipient the wrong way, but that was fine by me. You might not love me but you were definitely going to remember me.

My shock and awe today tends to revolve around magic rather than mail. When you meet me for the first time and we exchange business cards, mine will automatically catch fire and immediately extinguish before I hand it to you. The shock and awe isn't the card catching fire as much as the fact that when the card hits your hands it's neither hot to the touch nor visibly burned. When I speak to an audience I'll employ a variety of first-impression-making magic. You might see me turn a $1 bill into a $100 bill, rip up a newspaper and restore it so it is good as new, or eat fire. Like Big & Rich and Scott Slater, I want people thinking, "I can't believe this guy is doing that." I want them thinking that for a couple of reasons:

1. *I know I have their attention.*
2. *I know I'll keep their attention because they are wondering what I will do next.*
3. *I know they'll remember me. You've got to be different or you'll be invisible.*

Your shock-and-awe marketing might involve a job search and could be as simple as a resume and cover letter—the shock and awe would be in how, when, and where it arrived. A former coaching colleague of mine who prefers to remain nameless executed perhaps the greatest shock-and-awe campaign in the history of job searches. An ambitious assistant coach at a small college, he learned that the head basketball coach at a conference rival had just been fired that day. After returning from an away game late at night, he jumped in his car and drove four hours in the middle of the night to the rival college. Upon his arrival, he convinced (bribed) a campus security guard to not only let him in the administration building but to let him into the president's office to drop off his resume and a handwritten cover letter! Mission complete, he immediately jumped back in the car and headed home.

The next morning, the president arrived at his office and was shocked to find the envelope with the coach's resume and cover letter. In awe of the coach's resourcefulness, he immediately phoned his first and only candidate to invite him to interview for the position (which the coach was offered and accepted). The story holds a powerful lesson for us all, because the college president's rationale in interviewing and hiring the coach was that if someone was willing to go to those extremes to land the job, imagine how hard he would work to keep the job and build the program into a winner. Sometimes great opportunities are born of great shock and awe.

A by-product of shock and awe is traction and media attention. "Save a Horse" became the theme song for ESPN's World Series of Poker program as well as the music in a Chevrolet commercial, and ten years after the song's release it made an appearance in the 2012 movie *Magic Mike*. A fusion of country rock and rap, the song has some broad appeal—and it went platinum—but I would contend that the secret sauce that gave it legs was the shock and awe of the video and the duo's live appearances.

YOU

What can you do to shock and awe decision makers or members of your audience into a great first impression? Perhaps you are typically a bit more conservative in your approach. In that case, shock and awe might take the form of sending a proposal in a FedEx overnight envelope instead of via snail mail or e-mail. It's an attention getter and the delivery method indicates that the contents are time sensitive enough to send overnight. Shock and awe could be adding a mascot to your business; sports teams have them for a reason. Mascots are friendly, approachable, and memorable for kids and adults of all ages. My client Nate Wadsworth is a member of the House of Representatives in Maine, and operates a fourth-generation family business in his community. His fifth great grandfather was an American officer in the Revolutionary War and the grandfather of Henry Wadsworth Longfellow. To showcase Wadsworth's family's roots in the community and use shock and awe when campaigning we hired a man to attend events dressed in a colonial costume. The costumed colonist held a campaign sign and handed out brochures. More important than the distribution of the marketing collateral, was the fact that the costumed colonist was highly approachable and a conversation starter—just like a sports mascot.

Like Nate Wadsworth's colonial campaigner, you want to stand out rather than fit in. Odds are, you aren't the only vendor or service provider in your market. If you are, congratulations—you're the rare exception. Your industry is probably a lot like the restaurant industry. There are lots of choices when it comes to getting a hamburger, and 99.9 percent of those choices are about the same. Price may vary a little but the product is similar. And then there's a Slater's 50/50 burger. It's different, it's memorable, it's one of a kind, and it's talked about. A lot. You want to be the Scott Slater of your industry so you aren't competing on price, but are providing a one-of-a-kind experience and making a memorable first impression.

Stadium Steps

1. In the blank space below, create a list of the most outrageous ideas that you'd never in a million years be comfortable doing. Circle the craziest one you want to rule out and never do.
2. Carry out the idea that you just circled.

PART III

Connection

CHAPTER 15

Focus on Your Fanatics

Fans don't boo nobodies.

—Reggie Jackson, professional baseball player

If I were a betting man, I'd bet that 80 percent of you *won't* execute what I'm about to share with you. And that's okay; this information is for the other 20 percent. You need to figure out if you're in the 20 percent or the 80 percent.

Let's start with some information gathering:

1. Write down the number of employees on your staff. Off the top of your head, write down the names of the ones who give you the most problems.
2. Write down the approximate number of clients in your book of business. Now, off the top of your head, jot down the names of the ones who account for most of the revenue.
3. To take it a step further, write down the number of salespeople on your team. List the names of the ones who bring in the most revenue.

Go back to the answers you wrote for the preceding exercise.

1. If you do some quick math, you'll find that roughly 20 percent of your employees cause 80 percent of your headaches.
2. On the flipside, about 80 percent of your revenue is coming from 20 percent of your clients.
3. You will also notice that 80 percent of your production is coming from 20 percent of your sales representatives.

Congratulations! In this simple exercise, you just experienced the power of the Pareto principle. Let me explain. Vilfredo Pareto was an Italian economist who, back in 1906, figured out that 80 percent of all land in Italy was owned by 20 percent of the citizens. He studied neighboring countries and found this phenomenon held true in the other countries as well. Pareto then determined that the phenomenon didn't hold true only in real estate or economics; it was a rule of thumb in every industry.

The Pareto principle states that 80 percent of your results will come from 20 percent of your actions. If you reflect on aspects of your life, you'll see it's a universal truth. Eighty percent of your productivity comes from 20 percent of your employees, 80 percent of your complaints come from 20 percent of your clients, 80 percent of your wealth comes from 20 percent of your investments, and so on.

With the Pareto principle in mind, there are two ways you can run your business: like U2 or like Eric Church.

Them

A huge victory for all entrepreneurs took place when Eric Church released his new album, *Mr. Misunderstood*, on November 4, 2015, at the Country Music Awards. Secretly, he released the album the day before by giving it as a gift to members of the "Church Choir," his fan club, but it didn't hit the iTunes music store until after the awards show had begun.

Church's release of his new album was a huge success, and the album sold 71,000 copies in the first thirty hours of availability alone, coming in at number three on the Billboard Top 100. Inside Church's counterintuitive strategy lies a huge lesson for all entrepreneurs.

First, the album's release was a total surprise. There was zero promotion, hype, or interviews leading up to the release, and Church's record label didn't even know he was producing the album. Church's stunt represents guerilla marketing at its finest. He had a street team passing out flyers announcing the release of his surprise album in downtown Nashville during and after the CMA awards show. His team also created a pop-up store in East Nashville that opened immediately after the show. And he partnered with Uber to create a special promotion that allowed fans to order a ride from Uber drivers whose car was playing the album.

Church's release of *Mr. Misunderstood* is a great example of disruptive marketing. The game has changed, and gone are the days of mass media advertising and traditional product launches. Given today's ADD culture and twenty-four-hour news cycle, you need to be different or risk being invisible. Church was not only different, he created more goodwill and word-of-mouth advertising than money could ever buy.

Many in advertising believe businesses are competing for "mindshare"; I would argue that you're far better off competing for "heart share" of your customers. Which is the more valuable place to be located: on their minds or in their hearts? Focus on impact, and you will drive income far better than if you focused merely on income and selling. By giving the album away as a gift to his fan club members, Church created heart share in the minds of all 80,000 of his fan club members. This is what happens when we stop thinking about selling all the time and start focusing on giving and overdelivering—and it's the best way to develop a critical mass of fans.

Freemium promotions drive impact and heart share. This model revolves around long-term thinking, looking ahead to the fifth sale, not merely shooting for one quick, immediate sale. It's not enough to tell your fans you love them; you've got to show them, like Church did. Entrepreneurs can learn a lot from Church's strategy. Are you building a sale or a sales career? The old rules of business don't apply anymore.

To take heart share a step further, Church didn't just paint a picture for his fans with an advertisement; he painted them into the picture with his surprise gift. And he even let one of them help paint the picture. Instead of putting himself on the album cover and video, Church put fourteen-year-old musician Mickey Smay front and center on both. And Smay doesn't just appear in the video, he essentially *is* Mr. Misunderstood. Smay also announced the release of the album at the CMA press conference on behalf of Eric Church.

You don't have to conform or do things the way everyone has always done them in your industry either. The album title and lead track, *Mr. Misunderstood*, is a concept we can all relate to. As entrepreneurs, we are often Mr. or Ms. Misunderstood. There's nothing normal about us. We think differently, act differently, and view the business world differently. We are also misunderstood because we hold ourselves to a standard and level of accountability in a way that is very different from the rest of our contemporaries.

We voluntarily log long hours and late nights, and we face unrelenting criticism for pursuing our passion on the path less traveled. Entrepreneurship, like music, is not a job—it's a way of life, an obsession, and a subculture unto itself. And if you're not one of us, you don't understand us. We are all misunderstood, and we probably wouldn't have it any other way.

It stands to reason that Church chose the path less traveled for the release of his album. He prides himself on being a self-proclaimed "outsider" in country music circles. There's a method to his stealth madness, and it's a method we would all be wise to follow.

When Church's fan club members received the album as a gift via a surprise snail mail package, it looked a little different than you'd expect. *Mr. Misunderstood* wasn't just any album; it was vinyl. And it wasn't just your run-of-the-mill black vinyl record, it was white vinyl. I've seen tons of vinyl records, but until Church's I'd never seen a white vinyl one. Vinyl alone is a great way to be different, but white vinyl? That's a stadium status move. Accompanying the album was a handwritten note from Church. In it he explained that every instrument has a story to tell and it's up to the keeper of the instrument to turn those stories into songs.

His fans also had a great story to tell as the packages started arriving on their doorsteps in the days leading up to the formal launch. Upon receipt, fans started tweeting about the surprise gift album they received, posting pictures on Facebook and Instagram, Periscoping live video of themselves listening to the new release, and just talking about it in person as well.

While what Church did was unique, what's equally significant is what he didn't do. He didn't ask his fans to promote the launch of the album, he didn't say in his letter, "I'm giving you a free gift, here's the value attached to it. In return what I'm asking you to do is tweet about it eight times, post it on Facebook twice, and tell twenty of your closest friends to go buy the album." He didn't ask for a thing, he just gave his music away to the very people who were most likely to buy it. And in return, his fans gave back to him tenfold.

Eric Church isn't just an artist, he is a brand. The lesson for every entrepreneur is that you, too, are a brand, and every brand has a story to tell. It's up to the entrepreneur to turn those stories into customers, and those customers into a stadium full of raving fans. The key to doing so successfully is all in the approach.

We blaze our own trail into the woods and hope people come along for the ride, but are we focusing on the right passengers? The right passengers are the first few fanatics—80,000 of them, in Church's case.

The Fanatical Few versus the Mediocre Many

In September of 2014, U2 partnered with Apple to force its new album, *Songs of Innocence,* on half a billion iTunes users. The release is believed to have been the biggest in history, but bigger isn't always better. In the process, U2 and Apple angered customers and damaged their respective brands by flooding the market with the musical equivalent of junk mail. I remember being annoyed that iTunes forced that album on me, and that I didn't know how to remove the album from my account (and I'm even a U2 fan).

The download was intended as a free gift, but Apple violated its customers' trust by invading their devices. I know I began thinking, if Apple can download an album to my device without me knowing, I can only imagine what else the company could do to my phone and my account. The entire move reeked of desperation.

Many critics and other musicians speculated that the once iconic band, which hadn't released an album in several years, was worried their brand was dying on the vine and gave the album away before it had an opportunity to flop in the stores. Was U2 operating out of fear? Did they feel they had to reach more people than ever before, new audiences that they had not previously appealed to? They were worried about broadcasting their message when they should have focused on narrowcasting it.

A broadcast is like a shotgun blast: not accurate. Narrowcasting is like a shot from a sniper rifle with a scope and a laser sight. Which is more accurate, a shotgun or a sniper rifle with a scope? I'll give you a hint: if Eric Church were a weapon, he'd be a sniper rifle and, unfortunately for U2, they'd be the shotgun.

When in Doubt, Look in Not Out

Church looked inward instead of outward and focused on his first few fanatics, his fan club members, who are his biggest ambassadors. U2 looked outward and, in the process, frustrated a large number of people who didn't want the band's music. Church refined his target audience to include only his biggest fans. It's what he has always done, and it's what you should do: play your music for the people who want to hear it most. It's the 80/20 rule executed perfectly.

In the case of Church's music, 80 percent of the support for his music will come from 20 percent of his audience—the most passionate 20 percent, his fan club. You can apply Pareto's wisdom to your business as well. Who are your biggest fans? How are you investing in them? Before you answer, let me lead by example.

Bru

In my past career as a college coach, I saw that 80 percent of our players came from 20 percent of the showcases, high schools, and junior colleges we visited. When I realized this, I doubled down and invested in developing deeper relationships with those institutions and coaches. Examining our talent acquisition activities made us more focused and productive, and saved us massive amounts of precious time and travel expenses. It also landed us more loyal and enthusiastic players, who bought into the system quickly and were some of our best recruiters when it came to signing new talent for the next class.

In my second career as a speaker and executive coach, I took the Pareto principle to a deeper level and I encourage you to do the same. After discovering that 20 percent of my clients were indeed responsible for more than 80 percent of my revenue, I went a step further and looked within that initial 20 percent to determine which of those clients were responsible for 80 percent of that revenue. These were my MVPs, or most valuable people, literally. Taken to a third level, 20 percent of my 4 percent would be .8 percent. Just .8 percent of my client base created 51 percent of my total revenue! I now dedicate a majority of my attention and resources to this handful of clients in the form of premium experiences, client appreciation events, gifts, and value-added services. This heightened focus has brought about new opportunities in the form of additional work within their organizations and referrals to their professional peers.

Developing your business in any other way is a colossal waste of time and energy. You should be preaching to your choir and allowing them the opportunity to sing your praises. Most entrepreneurs spin their wheels by investing the majority of their time trying to convert the uninterested masses into buyers, whether they are ideal clients or not. And they're usually not.

The term "fan" is, indeed, short for fanatic, which the *Oxford Dictionary* defines as "a person filled with excessive and single-minded zeal." The hidden value of fans lies in a certain subset of your fans called superfans. Superfans are the ones who own every single product your company makes or who consistently and frequently purchase the experiences your brand offers.

The Pareto principle applies to superfans as well. Nielsen research, published in "Turn It Up," a March 2013 article on Nielsen.com, indicates that 14 percent of music consumers account for 34 percent of all music spending. Nielsen refers to them as aficionado fans, and their purchases aren't limited to the music itself. These aficionados also buy artist merchandise, attend live concerts, and purchase premium streaming of music on sites like Pandora and Spotify.

What Nielsen also discovered was that the music industry was leaving a lot of money on the table when it came to aficionados. The same study revealed that US music fans spend between $20 and $26 billion on music each year. Where it gets interesting is in the fact that such fans disclosed that they could spend an additional $450 million to $2.6 billion annually if they had the opportunity to participate in behind-the-scenes experiences with the artists and receive premium exclusive content such as in-studio updates, limited editions, autographed handwritten lyric sheets, and vinyl albums.

Nielsen's research could be extrapolated from music and applied to just about any industry. Whether you realize it or not, a segment of your customer base is made up of aficionados or superfans. It's time you identify them and give them the attention they deserve. If the music industry gave its superfans the attention and access they wanted, the industry's revenue would increase by 10 percent ($2.6 billion). What could a 10 percent increase in revenue do for you?

Take a page from Eric Church by creating a fan club for your business. He offers what I call a good-better-best membership model. You can join his fan club, the Church Choir, for free at the basic level. This gives you access to Church's online community and his membership site. Standard annual membership ($19.95) includes the early access Nielsen spoke about: presale tickets, merchandise exclusives, Church Choir parties, and opportunities to meet Eric Church. And premium annual membership ($49.95) contains all elements of the basic membership and adds collectible merchandise in the form of a CD, T-shirt, bumper sticker, and drink koozie.

Church has created a win-win situation for everyone. He isn't alienating his superfans, he's providing them with the access and opportunities that research has proven they crave. It's important to note he was ahead of the curve and had been taking good care of his fans well before Nielsen's research came out. He is also maximizing his revenue opportunities, and with every customer touch point that takes the form of an experience, he can deepen the relationship he has with the fan. With every T-shirt and decal sold, potential new fans are exposed to the Eric Church brand. Your superfans are your best advertisers.

When I was coaching collegiate lacrosse, I created booster clubs with a similar good-better-best membership model that Church uses for his Church Choir. At each of my coaching stops, the booster clubs became our team's single greatest revenue stream, ahead of ticket sales, concessions, and any other fundraising activities we performed. Most years, my operating budget hovered around $35,000, and I was able to come close to doubling that figure through two initiatives: the booster club and a formal preseason banquet, to which booster club members received presale access to tickets. An interesting thing happened; very few members opted for the basic membership and more than 50 percent selected the premium in order to gain access to exclusive "superfan" merchandise. People will pay for access.

As a case in point: a parent of one of my players was a single mother of thirteen boys. The family had dirt floors in a home they built by hand in the backwoods of Maine, and the player received a ton of federal, state, and institutional financial aid. The mother purchased a booster club membership and took off work to come to every game. She loved the fact that the membership came with VIP parking next to the field and reserved front-row seating. It was one of the few luxuries in her life. For a couple of hours a week, we made her feel stadium status. Off the record, I will tell you she didn't receive one T-shirt and hat: I made sure I slipped twelve more into the package for each of her other kids, along with some extra bumper stickers she could share with her colleagues at work.

You

This chapter isn't about Eric Church, U2, or even me. This chapter is all about you. Do you see yourself in the U2 story? What I mean by that is, are you trying to go everywhere and be at every event because you think your absence is noticed more than your presence, and you're worried about public perception? Do you think you have to reach as many people as you can? Are you operating out of scarcity instead of abundance?

The best U2's *Songs of Innocence* did was chart at number nine outside the United States for a short period of time, and it was the band's first album that didn't go platinum. It didn't even make gold, which is only 500,000 albums. The game changed, and the band didn't evolve. It's not about broadcasting, it's about narrowcasting. Your business is the same way. There are more than seven billion people on planet Earth, and your message, product, or service isn't for everyone—but it absolutely is for a select few. Those few can be your biggest allies, and they can advocate for you in a way that no one else can.

You have to focus on your first few fanatics.

1. Name your superfans. Church has the Church Choir and Boston has Red Sox Nation. Mine are affectionately known as the Bru Crew, and I've created an inner circle membership site for my readers, clients, and audience members.
2. Create a social media hashtag for superfans that they can use; tweet about them and retweet them. You'll be seen as a person who is more authentic, accessible, and caring than your competition. Taylor Swift

affectionately calls her fan club members The Swifties and tags them on social media with #Swifties. It's searchable, ties them together, and lets her interact with them.

3. Show them love. Create special events for your fan club members and encourage them to bring a guest. While it may feel like extra work to socialize after hours with customers, there are few things more important than engaging with them. Whether it's a behind-the-scenes tour of your facility or a short chat to thank them and show you appreciate them, your time and attention will pay dividends. Don't look at this as a formality; shift your perspective. It's something you get to do, not something you have to. Interacting with your fans is an honor and a privilege. They will promote your services harder, they'll tell friends, and they'll even bring friends with them to events.

4. Remember that it's not about you. It's all about your fans. Without fans, authors, sports teams, and musicians have no career. Neither do you. You may be the one signing your employees' paychecks but it's your fans who pay their salaries. Don't ever let anyone in your organization forget this important detail. You have a responsibility to your fans. Sign handwritten notes to them, autograph items, and connect on a level that your competitors do not. The second that level of attention goes away, so do your customers. And then so does your business.

How are you painting your clients into the picture and letting them help paint the picture? Your industry is probably a lot like the music industry, crowded and commoditized. Who are the core group of fans who can help spread your message? Focus your efforts on the fanatical few instead of the mediocre many—it will pay off big time.

Stadium Steps

1. Find the fanatical few: 80 percent of your business comes from 20 percent of your clients.

   - Step 1: Calculate which of your clients are responsible for 80 percent of your revenue.
   - Step 2: Now dig deeper and look at the 20 percent within the 20 percent. Which of the 20 percent you identified in Step 1 are responsible for 80 percent of that 20 percent revenue figure?
   - Step 3: Repeat the process by calculating the top 20 percent of that 20 percent to reveal your VIP clients.

2. List several ideas for how you can dedicate greater attention and resources to these newly minted VIPs. (For example, create premium experiences, client appreciation events, or valued-added services.)

3. Extrapolate the Pareto principle beyond your revenue.

- Which marketing activities produce 80 percent of your results?
- How about your sales and prospecting activities?
- What is the one thing that generates the largest number of referrals for you?
- It's your turn: select an area of your business on which to apply the 80/20 rule.

CHAPTER 16

Low Tech, High Touch

Sending a handwritten letter is becoming such an anomaly. It's disappearing. My mom is the only one who still writes me letters. And there's something visceral about opening a letter—I see her on the page. I see her in her handwriting.

—Steve Carell, actor and comedian

In today's instant, on-demand, fast-paced, high-tech world, believe it or not: low tech wins. By low tech I'm referring to handwritten thank-you notes and letters. When I was a child, my mom always made me write a handwritten note to people who did something nice for me, gave me a gift, or made a difference in some way. It's a habit that I carried into adulthood, and it's one that I've passed along to my children.

One of the NFL's greatest quarterbacks, Peyton Manning, has done the same thing throughout his career, sending notes to retiring opponents he respects and admires. He, too, credits his mother for instilling the habit in him (I guess I'm in pretty good company). I'm struck by the thoughtfulness, humility, and respect for his profession that Manning has. Can you see yourself handwriting a letter to your competitors when they retire to let them know you appreciate the fact that they conducted themselves with class and integrity? How about to your customers and prospects? Is that too time-consuming or "low tech" for you?

Here are three compelling reasons that low tech wins:

1. It's a nice surprise when you go to the mailbox and find a handwritten note among the bills, junk mail, and magazines.
2. It's different and it sets you apart in what is otherwise a sea of sameness.
3. It demonstrates that you invested time in sending something from the heart.

I remember the first handwritten recruiting letter I received in high school. It was from Tom Gill, the head lacrosse coach at Fairleigh Dickinson University.

I got plenty of typed form letters from other coaches, but Gill's first contact with me was a handwritten note. He told me I'd be a great fit at FDU, encouraged me to visit the campus, and wished me a great senior year. He even added a PS at the bottom asking me to tell my high school coach, John Distler, that he said hello. It was the one recruiting letter I have kept, and as the recruiting process unfolded, wouldn't you know it, I ultimately ended up committing to play at FDU.

Them

In chapter 15, you saw the power of Eric Church's direct personal connection to his fans when compared with U2's shotgun blast approach. One communication was perceived as a nuisance, the other as a personal gift—and I don't even mean the album. As a member of the Church Choir, I know I valued the handwritten letter from Church even more than the album itself. Church's music can be bought anywhere, but what can never be purchased is the personal attention he gave his fan club members. The greatest gift we can give those we care about is the gift of our personal attention.

Today, there are more ways than ever to get someone's attention, between text messages, e-mail, and a multitude of social media platforms; as a result of the clutter, none of these methods stands out above all the others online. When you go offline, you'll elevate and separate yourself from the online clutter. There's no app for that, but there is a paper and pen. These two tools are the college coach's weapons of choice, and ought to be yours too. While it's certainly faster, easier, and more convenient to send an e-mail, people typically don't store special e-mails as keepsakes. But lots of people save and display handwritten notes.

Among the most treasured letters are the handwritten notes by Coach Jerry Wainwright, now associate head basketball coach at Fresno State University. Coach Wainwright, in what might be the most stadium status move of all time, wakes up at 3:30 every morning and spends about an hour and a half handwriting notes to his former players and the many coaches he knows. Coaches who receive a Wainwright letter with a motivational note or quote tend to keep them and display them. Some even collect them.

Jerry Wainwright began coaching in the 1970s and has been handwriting his basketball notes to people for about thirty years. While he's been a head coach at three different universities and led teams to the postseason seven times, Coach Wainwright has reached legendary status in the profession for his notes. More specifically, he's known for the level of thoughtfulness and care that go into each of his missives. The ability to personalize individual messages and share the right words of appreciation or support at the right time has a way of coming back to the sender tenfold. When DePaul University fired Wainwright as head basketball coach in 2010, he received hundreds of phone calls in support, a compelling example that when you do good, good will follow.

A handwritten note is not just a piece of paper with ink on it. Such a note is personalized, not mass produced, and it sends a strong message to the recipient that he is important to you. When you take the time to personalize the message, you demonstrate that you are making a thoughtful, purposeful gesture. E-mails and texts are, by nature, impersonal because they are all too often sent out by the thousands.

Bru

What do a country music star, a couple of college coaches, and a politician have in common? I know you're probably thinking that sounds like the beginning of a bad joke, but I assure you it's no joke. Keep reading, you're about to find out. Success leaves clues, and often the simplest strategies have the greatest effect. Notice I used the word "simplest," not "easiest." Handwriting notes daily is simple; you sit down, write the notes, seal the envelopes, and slap stamps on them. But—and that's a big but—there's nothing easy about it. It involves a significant level of attention, care, dedication, and investment of your time to execute. If it were easy, stories about musicians, NFL stars, and coaching icons (Wainwright, not me) handwriting letters wouldn't stand out as the stuff of legends.

Act One

I was fortunate that, when I started my coaching career, Al Gore hadn't yet invented the Internet. Technology and social media hadn't invaded every aspect of communication, creating clutter and destroying attention spans. When I began coaching, every aspect of our recruiting was done via snail mail. At that time, most recruiters opted for the easy method: have the secretary send a form letter or do a mail merge and send out a mass-produced letter. Sometimes our adversity is our advantage, though, and we only connect the dots when we look backward. I didn't have the luxury of a secretary, and I shared an office with eight other coaches. We all shared four desks, and, if that wasn't bad enough, we had only one computer among us.

The logistical nightmare of getting office work done led me to do two things. First, it gave me the hidden luxury of not using a computer to recruit. Most coaches, both then and now, have most of their recruiting done with the help of a computer. However, instead of using the mass-produced, impersonal "Dear Prospect" form letters most were sending, I handwrote letters and notes to prospects and their families.

Old-fashioned? Yes. Time-consuming? That depends. You could consider it either an expense or an investment, depending on how you look at it. I found that what initially seemed like adversity (lack of a computer) turned to advantage as time went on. A personal, handwritten letter carries way more clout and value to a prospect and his family than what is clearly a mass-produced form letter. With the former a coach demonstrates your value, while with the latter that coach is sending you a clear signal that you're simply being recruited by a computer.

This old-school strategy enabled me to gain access to prospects my competitors could not. Why? Because I did what they would not do—I went the extra mile and gave them personal attention. In response, I was rewarded with the opportunity to schedule a visit with the prospect's family in their home (think, sales call). Handwritten envelopes get opened more often than typed ones—it's really that simple.

Act Two

Early in my professional career I made handwritten correspondence a best practice, both as a recruiter and as a sales manager. Regardless of the industry you're working in, personal notes yield results. I still write them myself and I encourage all business leaders to do the same. What the handwritten note does is build equity with the recipient. E-mails get deleted. Handwritten notes are kept, often displayed and seen by numerous other people. I can't tell you how many times I've walked into a client's office and seen one of my handwritten notes or a thank-you card from someone pinned to the bulletin board. Take a look yourself the next time you walk into someone's office. I'd be shocked if you didn't see a few notes yourself.

Could you express the same thing via Skype or in an e-mail? Sure, but it won't have the same effect or carry the same emotion. Handwritten correspondence creates a strong level of social equity with the recipient. It's true that the recipient can't hit "reply" on a note card, but research indicates that a physical piece is processed on a more emotional level in the recipient's brain. If you think about it, a handwritten letter leaves an understandably deeper impression. According to research organization Mindlab International, this is because the parts of the brain that are stimulated in the process of reading the letter are the same parts responsible for making an emotional connection with the sender.

My coaching clients who have the greatest business growth attribute much of their success to this one simple activity. This isn't just a business-building strategy or a recruiting strategy; at its core, it builds relationships. One of my coaching clients, Representative Nathan Wadsworth, is a politician, and during his election campaigns the single most effective strategy he employed was sending a handwritten postcard to follow up on every interaction he had with voters he met on the campaign trail. He made this practice nonnegotiable, and scheduled note writing into his calendar every single day. And he continues to carry stamped postcards with him as a follow-up strategy. Simple? Yes. Powerful? No doubt. It is an investment of time that pays dividends. Would you rather invest a little more time with fewer people, knowing that your attention will yield a greater return? Or do you just want to take the most expeditious route, cross your fingers, and hope that blasting a message to the masses might land you a couple of customers? Don't answer that until you finish this next section.

You

Old-fashioned is the new high tech. Why? Because it works. Before you immediately dismiss that thought, follow me for a minute here. Let's walk through a hypothetical situation. Or, feel free to break out a calculator, insert your own numbers, and do the calculations specific to your mailing list.

Take a look at the number of subscribers you have in your database. According to Ross Lasley, Internet marketing expert and CEO of The Internet Educator Inc., the average open rate on e-mail newsletters is 15 percent. Lasley says this can vary slightly, depending on the size of your business and your industry or profession.

If you are using one of the more popular electronic newsletter platforms, an above-average open rate is approximately 20 percent. That's deceptive, because "open" doesn't mean that what you've sent actually was read by that 20 percent of your audience, it simply means that 20 percent of your list opened the e-mail. According to Lasley, the average click-through rate is 6 percent.

Let's assume you have 10,000 subscribers on your mailing list. An open rate of 20 percent indicates that 2,000 people opened the e-mail. They may not have actually read it, they simply opened it. Of that 2,000, only about 6 percent read your e-mail; they did not necessarily act on it, they simply read your e-mail. That's 120 people, and that's a pathetic number by anyone's standards.

Eight thousand people didn't open your e-mail, and 9,880 didn't read your message. Those numbers should be disturbing to everyone. That means that 9,880 subscribers who supposedly follow you have absolutely no idea what you're doing. On the flipside, if you received a handwritten letter with a stamp on it, would you open it? E-mails and voicemails are easy to ignore or delete, and phone calls are invasive (especially cold calls). Handwritten notes are hard to ignore, and with online bill pay, most people don't even receive hard copies of bills in the mail anymore. As a result, your handwritten envelope stands out even more in what has become a smaller snail mail inbox.

Do a little a lot. Brevity rules. If you simply block off the first thirty minutes of your day to engage in what I call my five by nine strategy, you and your business will be better because of it. Five by nine refers to the strategy of sending five handwritten notes to clients, prospects, coworkers, or colleagues by nine o'clock in the morning each day. Make it a nonnegotiable appointment with yourself every single day, like Representative Wadsworth did.

Stadium Steps to a Successful Handwritten Note

1. *Remember that weight and quality matter.* The weight, brightness, and overall quality of the paper are a reflection of the sender and should be congruent with the quality of the written message.
2. *Match the message to the medium.* Because research indicates that paper resonates more deeply with us emotionally, you should reserve your most emotional messages for the handwritten page.

3. *Consider the demographics of the recipient.* Handwritten notes tend to be a more conventional and comfortable form of communication for a baby boomer or Gen Xer than they are for a Millennial/Gen Y recipient.

4. *Take advantage of the staying power.* A handwritten note is more than a note; it's really a gift. A handwritten note has far greater staying power and will be shared with other people far more often than an e-mail. E-mail can be deleted more easily than a letter can be thrown away. Nothing will ever replace a handwritten note.

5. *Realize that it's personal.* A well-written letter can be more intimate and moving than a conversation. It can be more touching and emotive than a phone call.

6. *Reinforce Brand YOU.* Make sure you make a brand impression on the recipient by including your logo, and perhaps even a photo, as well as your contact information on the card.

7. *Sustain your focus and engagement.* A handwritten note requires you to concentrate on your message and how you want to convey it. There's no backspace or delete key.

8. *Invest in a good pen and penmanship.* Your recipients can't love it if they can't read it.

9. *Don't use a signature stamp.* It's lazy and it's obvious. All the recipient has to do is wet her fingertip and rub it across your signature. If it smears right away she will know you cut that corner and used a stamp.

PS: Include a PS. Nothing adds value quite like that final statement. In psychology, there is a concept called the recency effect, which essentially states that your mind will find the last thing you see, hear, or read to be most memorable. It's trumped only by the primacy effect, which refers to the first thing you read. In other words, our brains are wired to remember the first and the last things that make impressions on us. So be sure to lead and conclude with your best stuff, and keep the message short and sweet.

CHAPTER 17

Let the Low Ride Go

It is not a daily increase, but a daily decrease. Hack away at the inessentials.
—Bruce Lee, actor and martial artist

Sometimes we complicate winning and, as a result, we don't enjoy as much success. Often, a better result isn't about adding something, it's about getting rid of something. In my work as a performance consultant, I frequently get phone calls from athletes, coaches, or executives who are looking for help because they're feeling stuck or they aren't experiencing the results they know they are capable of. Sometimes I even get late-night meltdown calls from people reaching out to me because they feel hopeless and they can't seem to reach their potential no matter what they do.

Nearly every time I've worked with an athlete who was in a slump or an executive whose business was struggling, the problem wasn't lack of effort. Rather, their struggles usually resulted from them attempting to do too much. A slump can take hold when an athlete or entrepreneur is adding strategies, overthinking, and/or utilizing new equipment. As a result, performance doesn't just flatline or fail to improve, it actually gets worse. The reason is simply that these "additions" create physical and mental clutter. Mental baggage weighs us down and slows our performance. We can achieve more by doing less, and there's a lesson to be learned from some iconic brands that understand that, whether you're selling an experience or lingerie, there's tremendous value in eliminating the nonessential.

Them

Simple is powerful, and sometimes the most important piece of simplification is knowing what to let go of. During a family vacation to Walt Disney World, I put myself in timeout while my wife and kids waited in line to ride Space Mountain. Probably much to Disney's disappointment, I'm one of those people who doesn't like roller coasters. Instead, I opted to chat up one of the managers in our area of the theme park. When I told him I didn't like roller coasters his response was, "Well, that's good to know." I asked him what he meant by that, and I learned that Disney has a meter for attendance on every single ride at the park. Every quarter, they examine the attendance numbers and remove from the park the lowest-attended ride. They call this concept "Let the Low Ride Go"—they are essentially eliminating the lowest-value activity from the park.

What I immediately began thinking was, "Why am I not doing this same thing in my business?" When we returned to our hotel room at the Disney resort that night, I began formulating my own version of the "let the low ride go." The idea didn't come to me overnight, but I decided that the most beneficial thing I could do for my business would be to fire some of my clients. While this may initially sound counterintuitive, firing my lowest-value clients actually improved my business. The bottom 20 percent of my roster, as you might guess, accounted for 80 percent of my headaches. These clients weren't as coachable or accountable, and they were not my ideal audience. I found that the time I freed up led me to more high-value opportunities.

In 2014, Victoria's Secret eliminated its mail-order catalog. Surprisingly, or perhaps not so surprisingly, sales increased by 40 percent. Victoria's Secret let its low ride go, and in doing so was better able to cater to its core customer. The revenue increase makes sense, if you look a little deeper.

When a customer buys an item at a Victoria's Secret retail store or via its website, the store gets the customer's e-mail address at the point of sale, and moving forward is better able to focus its marketing message directly to that decision maker. The e-mail marketing campaign is like a sniper's rifle, targeting interested customers, and the mail-order catalog was like a shotgun blast, trying to hit everyone at once. Between print costs, postage, and the fact that the catalogs weren't guaranteed to land in the hands of the target buyers in the homes they were mailed to, the mail-order business was a really expensive shotgun blast with a poor return on investment. I bet if you look a little closer at your marketing activities, like Victoria's Secret did, you'd find a way to recalibrate your efforts to more accurately target your ideal clients.

Bru

In 2013, I gave a speech to the members of the CEO Club of Boston. During the first hour of the conference, before I went on stage, the group conducted mastermind sessions at each table. Participants were divided into groups of four and asked to share with their group a situation or problem plaguing their business that month. Each of the situations presented at my table revolved around one theme: delegation—or, more accurately, a reluctance to delegate. One executive was reluctant to delegate key revenue-producing activities to the VP of sales, another felt he needed to micromanage the talent acquisition process for the human resources department, and a third was struggling to identify what uniquely differentiates her company from its competition.

Because I'm a performance consultant, my fellows at the table turned to me for expert solutions. My advice was simple and the same for each situation: let the low ride go. The first two CEOs could have benefited from delegating internally and the third could've benefited from outsourcing that challenge, hiring a marketing consultant to help her see the forest for the trees.

These CEOs were all experiencing is a common trap that many people fall into. Too often, we conduct our day-to-day operations in a certain way because we've always done it that way, or perhaps because we are simply afraid not to do them. You don't have to be a chief executive for this to sound familiar. Are you doing things simply because you've always done them, or because you're afraid not to do them?

Letting the low ride go is something I began doing in my business in 2010, and I have made it an annual event ever since. At the start of the year, I make a list of all my revenue-producing activities, take the top three, and commit to focusing on them exclusively. After I did this exercise for the first time, I hired an assistant and delegated every administrative activity to her. When necessary, I hire specialists to handle things like graphic design and product marketing. This strategy isn't about laziness; it's about eliminating the unnecessary so you can be more efficient and effective. By simply focusing on my top three revenue-producing activities (speaking, writing, and consulting), I've tripled my revenue—and that includes the expense of hiring outside talent. This strategy was game changing for me, and I believe it can be for you as well.

How, and how often, do you monitor your activity to gauge its effectiveness? Gone are the five-year plans; we are in the era of the five-minute plan. You can't afford to take a slow, wait-and-see approach. Most organizations no longer have the luxury of time—the stakes are too high and the competition too fierce in today's competitive market.

There's a lot you can learn by taking what I like to call "the coach approach" to your team's leadership. The coach approach involves examining your team's performance like a coach in a stadium assesses and addresses his team's performance on the field.

One of the coaches I respect most is Pittsburgh Pirates manager Clint Hurdle. Hurdle brought me in to speak to the organization's coaching staff during 2016 spring training. While I was there, I saw firsthand the Pirates' own version of the let-the-low-ride-go concept. It's a three-step, twenty-four-hour performance cycle Hurdle and the Pirates use to evaluate themselves daily.

1. Prepare
2. Execute
3. Review.

They prepare as a staff for the upcoming practice, then the execution phase takes place during the actual practices, and at day's end they perform their review. The review essentially lets the low ride go every single day. By quickly eliminating whatever isn't working, the team is better able to create incremental gains on and off the field. The beauty of the three-step cycle, for both the team and for your business, is the responsiveness—when you get immediate, daily feedback, you don't have time for things to fade from memory and you don't allow the clock to tick too long on mistakes that could become costly if not addressed quickly.

You

Your business is more like a sports team than you may think. Your performance is measured on a scoreboard of sorts, there's a sense of urgency, and to get ahead of the competition you've got to work smarter and harder. Responsiveness is a competitive advantage, and implementing a simple three-step performance review cycle can help you gain ground fast.

Let's look first at your business development strategies. When most of my clients begin working with me, they are dabbling in way too many different strategies instead of executing a few tried-and-true strategies and measuring the results.

One of the strategies I have them execute—and one I am encouraging you to implement—is Warren Buffett's 5/25 strategy. Make a list of all the business development strategies you have in place. Take the top five and separate them from the bottom twenty. Then let the bottom twenty go, because they aren't as valuable as the top five—and even thinking about them, much less acting on them, will pull your focus away from your top five.

Get your people to do more of what they are doing well. Too often, I see organizations require their salespeople to fill out lengthy sales activity reports, crunch numbers and make in-depth projections, update customer and prospect information in the company's online CRM system, and process orders. You'd never see a coach put a player in a position that doesn't play to his or her strengths. The goalie on my team never played offense, and I'd never ask my top midfielder to play in the goal. Both these moves would be wastes of time, and there would likely be a bad result because playing an unsuitable position doesn't exploit either person's strengths. Why, then, do so many organizations ask employees to operate outside their strengths? The answer is that it's the way they've always done things or they're afraid not to do them that way.

I'm encouraging you to do as I did and identify the top three revenue-producing activities of every employee and then free people up to focus exclusively on those activities. Take the sales department of your company, for example. Let's say that the average sale for one of your representatives is a $15,000 order. Why would you ask that salesperson to sit in her office updating a customer's contact information or processing an order when you could have her out in the field making more sales? The office work could be outsourced or delegated to an administrative professional, and two or three additional orders by that sales rep would pay the admin person's annual salary.

Early in my work with a former client, a health care organization that will remain nameless, one of the physicians commented to me that he was wasting time each week creating an Excel spreadsheet of his department's billing. His exact words were, "They're essentially paying me $250,000 a year to spend 20 percent of my time doing the job an administrative assistant could and should be doing." And the assistant would most likely do a better job with the spreadsheet, I might add. The reason an administrative assistant wasn't doing that work was, essentially, because this was the way the organization had always done things. I couldn't help but imagine how much more time the doctors in every department could've spent seeing patients and in turn driving revenue if they didn't have to fill out a weekly spreadsheet.

Sometimes we need a second opinion, a dose of reality, and a new prescription of sorts to get out of our own way and let the low ride go. Here is yours . . .

Stadium Steps

1. Which clients represent the "low ride" for you? List them and then let them go gently.

2. Make a list of your top revenue-producing activities and have each of your employees do the same. Commit to executing only your top three to five activities. Delegate or outsource all others. Track your revenue for the remainder of the fiscal year and compare the before-and-after revenue results.

3. Borrow a page from the playbook of Clint Hurdle and the Pittsburgh Pirates, and commit to the three-step performance cycle each and every day: prepare, execute, and review.

4. Huddle up with your team and put together your version of Warren Buffett's 5/25 list. It's okay if you can't come up with a total of twenty-five items; the point is to engage and get clarity on your highest-value activities so you can focus on those and eliminate the unnecessary ones.

5. Create a plus-one, minus-two policy. In my business, before I agree to add any activity, project, or task to my work routine, I eliminate two others. If the task is important enough to add, it had better be more important than at least two other activities I'm already involved in.

CHAPTER 18

Making Up When You Mess Up

Your most unhappy customers are your greatest source of learning.
—Bill Gates, American businessman, investor, and philanthropist

Customers have a very low tolerance for frustration today because they have so much more control than ever before. People don't merely accept things as they are or buy "off the rack" anymore. Customers expect to be in control of the buying experience; they expect to have their purchases—including the method of purchase and the delivery time—custom tailored to their demands. Think about the last time you bought an entire album rather than purchasing specific tracks on iTunes or creating your own curated playlist on Spotify. You can custom design your own station on Pandora based on your listening tastes to ensure you get exactly what you want. Commercial free, I might add.

It seems we've reached a point where even instant gratification takes too darn long for our liking. While most transactions today are practically instant and customer controlled, others remain embedded in processes with a lot of moving parts where the customer has little to no control. Mortgage buying comes to mind as an example of a complicated transaction over which the consumer has limited control. If you're in an industry, like the mortgage business, where your customers are "flying blind," here's something helpful to remember: people determine whether they can trust you based on whether or not you do *what* you said you would do *when* you said you would do it and *how* you said you'd do it.

Them

On June 25, 2016, Kenny Chesney was performing a concert at Lincoln Financial Stadium in Philadelphia. He gave a shout-out to Christopher Dorman, a local fan who couldn't be in attendance. Officer Dorman of the Folcroft Police Department couldn't attend the show because he was in surgery after being shot seven times in the line of duty the night before. From his hospital bed,

Dorman posted a short video on Facebook thanking the first responders and doctors. He then said, "And, hey, Kenny, please don't forget about me."

The video made its way to Chesney, and while he was on stage that night Chesney gave Dorman a shout-out and mistakenly informed the crowd of about 50,000 people that Officer Dorman had died.

Initially, the gesture was a great moment of connection between Chesney and his audience because it added a personal touch to the performance. The fact that he would educate himself on current events going on in the local community and would take a moment to honor a police officer was touching. Lots of entertainers roll into a city and perform their standard show, which is the same in one city as it is in the next. Very few personalize the experience and acknowledge something significant that happened in the community.

Then the moment unraveled. Chesney mistakenly explained that Dorman died in the hospital. We've all stumbled over our words or mistakenly said something we wish we hadn't, we just don't usually do it over a live microphone in front of an audience of 50,000. While we may not be making our mistakes over a live mic amplified through stadium speakers for everyone present to hear, our customer service mistakes, communication gaffes, and other errors can become amplified to a level far greater than a live audience of 50,000. Social media has the ability to amplify messages to an exponentially greater audience, and the message will leave a permanent footprint online.

You can definitely tell a lot about more a company by the way it fixes mistakes than the way it behaves when things go well. We are living in an era where your recovery is more noteworthy than your delivery.

Sometimes, recovery is as simple as a quick solution, while at other times a heartfelt apology is needed. And then there are occasions when you really need to go the extra mile. What if you always went the extra mile? Why should you? Because most people won't. Holding yourself to a higher standard when you screw up will put you back at the top, even though your proverbial stock just dropped.

The best brands deliver more than expected when it comes to recovery. Why go above and beyond to do more than is expected? Because word of mouth can make you or break you; exceeding expectations will also reduce your churn rate and, most importantly, it creates an amazing window of opportunity. When you answer a customer's concerns and then some, you are afforded an opportunity to deepen the relationship, cement greater loyalty, and demonstrate in a very tangible way your appreciation of your customers.

What did Chesney do for Officer Dorman to make up for his mistake? A lot. He called him personally to apologize, wished him a speedy recovery, and thanked him for his service. Chesney didn't stop there, though; he also invited Dorman to a football game and out for a round of beers when he was fully recovered.

This is a textbook example of how to turn a loss into a win for your brand. The deepening of the relationship turned a customer into an even bigger fan. Acting to make up for your mistakes with humor and generosity enables you to convert a public relations disaster into a public relations coup. You don't have to be an entertainer to do this—you just need genuine care. If you were to spin a story or situation and manipulate the media, your gesture to the customer would come off as disingenuous . . . because it was. Make sure your heart is in the right place when you're in recovery mode.

If you're entering a new market or calling on a client or prospect in an unfamiliar town, it behooves you to get your finger on the pulse of the community. Learn its traditions, find out the cultural ethos of the community, and bring yourself up to speed on the current events taking place there. By doing your homework, you demonstrate a genuine interest in both your prospect and the community he proudly calls home. If you don't do your homework or don't genuinely show interest, your effort will seem like a contrived way to ingratiate yourself to your prospect, and it will do more harm than good.

Bru

We recently bought a new house. The real estate agency and mortgage company we hired are both owned by a client turned friend, Loni Graiver.

I don't think I've met a CEO who is harder on himself than Graiver, and I mean that in a good way: he holds himself and his company to a very high standard. An incredibly successful entrepreneur, Graiver has built the largest privately owned real estate agency in the state. He also doesn't "read his own newspaper clippings." Graiver is always looking to improve, as evidenced by the following update shared with his team at the end of the week. I was so struck by it, I got his permission to share it:

> While I could easily talk about all the successful closings Cumberland County Mortgage closed in June (and it was a record-breaking month), instead my post is focusing on the handful of transactions that we have missed closing dates on and thus, didn't deliver. So what did we do? Pay for added rent, pay for moving trucks, pay for the nicest hotel rooms, pay for storage units, send movers, send dinners, send cleaners, and anything else we could do to make up for delays due to crazy high volume. We feel that you can tell a lot more about a lender by how we repair our mistakes than how we act when all goes perfectly. I thank our hard-working processing team for all the extra hours put forth and our loan officers who all care about pleasing their clients far more than their paychecks. Good times ahead!

I can attest to Cumberland's practices, because my new home was one of the delayed closings. The beauty of Loni Graiver's post was that, earlier that year, I delivered a series of workshops to his agents where we specifically addressed ways to go the extra mile so they could elevate and separate themselves from the competition. The agents took it to another level and are executing these strategies both when closings go according to schedule and when there are delays in the process.

Customers expect transactions to be delivered instantly and seamlessly. When they're not flawless, you'll hear about it. Being proactive about problems and letting customers know in advance how you're going to make it up to them is the equivalent of preventive medicine for your business.

Think about the reasons you've stopped doing business with someone. The person or company probably screwed something up and didn't make any attempt to recover from the mistake, other than maybe saying, "I'm sorry."

In 2016, I hired a company to do some project management for my business. The employee who was assigned to my account, Jessica, screwed everything up from start to finish. There were typos, missed phone appointments, items miscategorized, incorrect pricing, and missing bar code numbers, to name just a few errors. When I confronted her with her mistakes, Jessica very condescendingly and dismissively said, "It's common in this business, you'll get used to it." I told her that would not be the case, and asked her to fix the errors while letting her know I would resolve the matter with her employer directly. At no time during the call did she accept responsibility for her mistakes or issue anything even vaguely resembling an apology.

At that point, I sent a detailed e-mail with my list of concerns and complaints to the owner of the company and followed up with a phone call to him. When I described the situation, his immediate response was, "That's pretty normal and is why we have your extra set of eyes to catch details like that." I assured him I wasn't born yesterday and that it was not normal. He asked, "Remind me again, which one of my employees was this?" (making it obvious that he didn't care enough to read my e-mail carefully or listen to the name I mentioned at the top of the call).

When I reminded him that the employee concerned was Jessica, his response was, "Oh, good." To which I said, "What do you mean? Nothing about my experience was good in any way? Why would you say that?" He responded, "She's resigned to take another position and her final day is at the end of the month." Clearly, this wasn't his first complaint about her, and he was relieved there wasn't a second problem employee he'd have to deal with.

He didn't say, "I'm sorry you've had a poor experience with Jessica, please know this is not the norm for our company. I hope you'll let us prove that to you moving forward." There was no mention of prorating my bill or comping me for all my wasted time and the headache his employee caused either. That was the day that company lost my business permanently.

You

Are you doing something *to* your customer or *for* your customer? It's the difference between manipulation and facilitation. And make no mistake about it, there's a big difference between the two. One gets you referrals, the other gets you fired. Going back to Loni Graiver's post, his final comment about his staff caring more about pleasing their clients than their own paychecks wasn't a platitude. In an era when most people don't walk their talk or put their money where their mouth is, Graiver's team does. If you're approved for a mortgage with Cumberland, Graiver's team will give you a $100 credit card for you to use to get another rate quote from a competitor. That's how confident Cumberland is that it is giving you the best mortgage deal possible—and when the team encourages you to get a second opinion, they are putting their best foot forward and establishing trust.

Let that sink in for a minute. Think about it like this: would your doctor pay for you to get a second opinion? Would a car dealer ever encourage you to go somewhere else and comparison shop? I believe we all know the answer to those questions. You can take a page from Cumberland's book by creating a policy that preauthorizes your employees to spend (invest) a designated amount of money to ensure the customer is happy. This practice sends a powerful message to your customers about just how much you value them and an equally powerful message to your people about just how much you trust their judgment.

It takes exponentially more time, energy, and money to replace a disgruntled customer with a new one than it does to retain an existing customer. By examining your churn rate (aka customer attrition or turnover) and multiplying that by your customer acquisition cost, you'll quickly see just how much more you spend replacing customers who have left you than you would've invested in nurturing your relationship with an existing customer and ensuring her happiness.

Do your people care more about pleasing their clients than their own paychecks? Loni Graiver's company motto is "Creating Relationships for Life," and I can attest to that. When our Realtor, Kim Fowler, was showing us houses my wife and I really liked a particular home. She could've easily just gone along with our decision, made a sale, and gotten her commission. Instead, she stepped in and talked us out of it, saying, "I won't let you make a bad decision and purchase something I know we are going to end up selling sooner rather than later. I want you in your dream home and in a home that I can help you make money on when you sell it years from now." Not only did she have our best immediate interest at heart, she was looking out for us long term. Creating a relationship for life, indeed!

What are the most common difficult conversations your employees have with your clients? Do they lose their voice or do they step up and push back on the client with their best interest in mind?

No matter how fabulous your product is or how excellent your customer service, it's inevitable that you'll have an unhappy customer or that a member of your team will make a mistake in execution. It's the customers who don't let you know they are unhappy that can really hurt you; the ones who voice their displeasure are a blessing, because there's something you can do to right the wrong and repair the relationship.

One way to persuade people is to drop f-words on your upset customers—no, not those words. Keep reading. For the first forty-five years of my life I hated mangos; they're too sweet and I dislike the taste, smell, appearance, and even the texture of the fruit. I swore I'd never eat them and would go to my grave hating them, but that all changed one day when I was visiting my friend Brian in Dallas. While I was staying at his house, he was snacking on dried fruit and said, "You've gotta taste these, they're amazing."

I said, "What is it?"
"Dried mango."
"No thanks, I hate mango," I said.

Brian laughed and said, "I understand. For the longest time I didn't like mango either, same with kiwi, papaya, or any exotic fruit, for that matter. Then my friend Jason had me try dried mango and it was an absolute game changer for me. Here, just take one bite." And he handed me a small slice out of the bag.

So, of course I took a bite, and at that moment the lightbulb went on over my head, bells rang, glitter and confetti dropped from the ceiling, and so began my newfound love of dried mango. Call it wizardry or a Jedi mind trick, but my friend Brian used the age-old Feel-Felt-Found technique. It is an empathy-building technique that helps you remove customer objections and reduce concerns.

Feel: Exhibit empathy by demonstrating that you understand how the other person feels.
Felt: Let the person know you've walked a mile in his shoes and once felt the same way.
Found: Explain to the person in a detailed way how you discovered that your concern or objection was inaccurate.

Let me demonstrate the technique for you with a common example I hear in my business:

Prospect: We don't invest in corporate training because it's too expensive.
Bru: I understand why you feel that way. When I was a sales manager, I felt the price of bringing in a corporate trainer was a little too high. But I realized that if the training helped, at a minimum, one sales rep make one additional sale, I found it paid for itself twenty times over. That's a return on investment that management was thrilled with.

You can apply Feel-Felt-Found to just about any industry, interaction, or situation; in or outside of business. It's a life skill as much as it's a strategy for addressing customer objections.

Stadium Steps

1. Create a culture of accountability: "When our team drops the ball on a client (makes a mistake, misses a deadline, causes an error, etc.) we will . . ." This is how we ensure that we do what we said, when we said we'd do it and how we said we'd do it.
2. List the most common difficult conversations your team needs to have with clients that don't happen consistently.
3. Consider: How are you creating relationships for life with your clients? Here's how you can impress upon your people the lifetime value of a customer: at the next staff meeting, have a team member calculate the average sale multiplied by the average number of purchases per week, month, and year times the average number of years a customer will do business with you.

   When they see the hard numbers, your team will understand that the company isn't just losing one sale when a customer leaves unhappy.
4. Set alerts. An extremely effective and underutilized way to get and keep your finger on the pulse of your clients and their community is to create Google Alerts for your clients' names and their businesses' names. When something good or bad happens involving them you're immediately notified by Google.

CHAPTER 19

On Tour

If you want to grow, be open to criticism.
—Kathy Mattea, American country music and bluegrass artist

There may be thirty-one flavors at your local ice cream shop, but most are just variations of vanilla. And the ice cream shop is really the only place vanilla sells. In an era when consumers can make their own playlists by purchasing individual tracks on iTunes and can design their own dress shirts to be delivered to their door, both customization and the customer are king. If you don't listen to your customers, someone else will. Now, more than ever, it's critical that you be connected to your stakeholders to learn and understand the things that matter most to them.

Walk into virtually any store and look at the shelves, and you'll see products getting lost in a sea of sameness. Ask a clerk to differentiate one product from another, and often he can't. It is said that a confused mind doesn't buy. A confused mind can't help sell your product either. This leaves most brands to compete on price, which is a race to the bottom—and a race virtually everyone loses. Tragically, that is how most businesses try to compete in every industry. What can you do to avoid this commoditization trap? One simple thing: hit the road. Literally, go on tour.

Visiting clients on a listening tour is the single greatest success strategy I teach my coaching clients. It's an idea I got from one of the most historic and iconic teams in all of sports, the Boston Red Sox.

Them

For a number of years right after John Henry's ownership group took control of the Red Sox, the front office diligently kept their ears to the ground by listening to their most important customers, the fans. At season's end, front office personnel would travel from Portland to Providence and everywhere in between holding town hall–style events. They called it their listening tour.

These listening tours were viewed by Red Sox management as a fundamental operating principle. Members of the Red Sox front office would listen to questions, feedback, and ideas from members of "Red Sox Nation," who are arguably the most passionate fans in professional sports. Additionally, they fielded comments and questions via webcast and posted the listening tour videos on their website.

Key ideas that have been implemented as a result of listening tour feedback are gluten free–food vendors, new ticket sale policies, and social media embedded into the ballpark experience. A listening tour, when paired with strong implementation based on feedback, can also be a powerful way to elevate and separate yourself from the competition.

One company that executes the listening tour strategy to perfection is Anderson Bean Boot Company. The company's general manager, Ryan Vaughan, is a colleague, friend, and, coincidentally, a longtime Red Sox fan. Vaughan shared with me how the Anderson Bean Boot Company uses listening tours to differentiate itself from its competition.

Vaughan created his own version of the listening tour by hiring tech reps to be the eyes and ears on the floor with the retailers that sell the company's boots. The reps don't visit the retailers to sell, just to listen and help. Vaughan mentioned that having tech reps visit retailers is very different from simply sending sales reps. A sales rep is typically looking for the next order, whereas the tech reps are listening and helping to find solutions for the retailer. Absolutely no selling involved. (Think of their store visits as reconnaissance missions where they gather intel.)

Key questions that get answered on the tour are:

- What trends are you noticing in the market?
- What's working for the competition?
- What can we do to make it easier for you to sell our boots?
- Who are our strongest competitors?
- When we lose a sale, who is it usually to?

A great example of listening in order to problem solve for the retailer and differentiating itself as a brand came when Anderson Bean created custom designs for specific retailers. The custom boots help the individual retailer distinguish itself from local competitors and simultaneously prevents Anderson Bean from becoming commoditized. The company has taken the listening tour to a higher level by holding trunk shows that allow customers to set an appointment to be fitted for a custom pair of boots. This provides the customer with the best possible level of service, and at the same time shows the retailer what its customers really want.

The leadership team at Anderson Bean really walks the talk. CEO and co-owner Traynor Evans literally walks the factory floor every day and stops to listen to his employees. Management offices are deliberately located inside the factory rather than next door, so that managers can be accessible and listen closely. It's a daily listening tour with internal customers. When was the last time you checked in with your employees to ask for feedback or suggestions that would improve their experiences?

Vaughan has also flipped the listening tour on its head by bringing retailers in to the factory to experience the production process. They spend two to four days at a time on site in Mercedes, Texas, being shown product, manufacturing, and designs. They are entertained during their visit, and at dinner Vaughan and his team make it a point to simply listen and learn. Many retailers look forward to their site visit and return every year.

Bru

Former client turned friend and colleague Derek Volk uses a variation on the listening tour. Volk is the president of Volk Packaging Corporation in Biddeford, Maine. Each year, Derek takes the first three weeks of January and embarks on a thank-you tour, traveling to visit each client with one simple mission: to look the clients in the eye, face to face, and personally thank them for doing business with his company. This personal touch results in a rapport that allows him to ask, how can we serve you better in the new year? There is no hidden agenda to upsell, cross sell, or get referrals. He simply wants to show his appreciation and deepen the client relationship to the point that each customer feels valued and respected, and also feels comfortable enough to share any concerns or constructive feedback she may have.

Founder and former CEO Ken Volk performs a similar listening tour for the company each summer, visiting key accounts to simply listen and learn about the client's business and to understand how he and his organization can better serve the client. Derek shared with me that the Volk Packaging customers look forward to Ken's visits, and often share feedback with Ken that they wouldn't necessarily share with their sales representative.

The first quarter of the fiscal year and the summer aren't slow times for Volk Packaging. The company is busy year round and, if anything, the first quarter is one of the busiest times. The fact that owners schedule their listening tours during busy times sends a strong message that they are invested in clients and the clients will always be priority number one.

The Red Sox management, too, conducts most of their listening tour during the front office's busiest time of the year, from November 1 through the holidays. This is the time when player acquisitions happen. Amid free agency, trades, and coaching changes, the front office and ownership invest time in getting out and listening to their customers. This sends a very clear message that they are never too busy to listen to their customers.

Often, in business, when we enter our busy season, we develop a bunker mentality and get so busy we forget to invest time in listening. Is a listening tour easy? No, but when you do the hard things the right way you set a solid foundation upon which you can grow.

When I was a college coach, my listening tour took place in the fall each year. The weeks just after back-to-school was an ideal time to schedule visits with high school coaches and guidance counselors during the day and then visit recruits and their families at their homes in the evenings. I would typically schedule weeklong tours in each of these areas: New England, New York City area/New Jersey/Long Island, Maryland/Virginia, and Upstate New York. It wasn't the most convenient time for me, but it was the most convenient time for my audience.

In my business now, I perform listening tours in the summer. Things tend to slow down a bit in my clients' businesses during the summer months, and they have more time available to visit with me. If they want to get out of the office and play golf, that's what we do. If they prefer to stay on site, we do that. The meetings are scheduled for their convenience, not mine, and that begins with respecting their time.

You

None of the businesses I've referenced in this chapter competes on price, mine included. Red Sox tickets won't be the cheapest in major league baseball, nor are they the least expensive entertainment in the Boston area. Anderson Bean's boots, Volk Packaging's boxes, and my speaking/coaching fees aren't competing on price either. We all differentiate based on relationships, quality, and the experience we offer.

You shouldn't be competing on price either. Your competitors can always offer a lower price, and if your response is to discount your service or product deeper than the competition you've already lost because you've devalued your brand. Competing on price is a race to the bottom, and it's one you don't want to win. Instead of lowering your price, raise your value. When prospects tell you that the company "doesn't have sufficient funds" in its budget to pay your fee, what they are really saying is you haven't shown them sufficient value to warrant them making that investment. By listening to prospects' needs more carefully, asking better questions, and helping them understand the value of your unique solution, you'll be better able to build the relationship and turn those prospects into clients. You will be compensated at a higher level than competitors when your prospects and clients understand that you deliver a level of value that is unparalleled, and that they can't get the kind of results you deliver anywhere else.

Perhaps your client base is one that is so fragmented and scattered about the country (or world) that a physical listening tour isn't feasible. If that's the case, take a page out of my friend Cowboy Troy Coleman's playbook. In June of 2015, Coleman sent country music fans an online music consumption preference survey. The purpose was to gauge his fans' preferences, to learn where and how they like to get their music, and that short, easy-to-answer online survey to listeners gave him incredible insight into how to better serve them. He received feedback almost immediately; within six hours, he'd captured information from the first hundred respondents from thirty-one different states and three Canadian provinces.

By asking fans where and how they get their music, Coleman gained a better understanding of how to market his products (CDs, digital music, live events, and merchandise) and where to place them. For example, he shared with me that 67 percent of his fans don't have a physical copy of his music, and this fact revealed to him a greater need to promote digital downloads of his music. The most interesting feedback he received was that 62 percent of his fans are willing to travel up to 100 miles to see a show. This caused him to take a closer look at the map and realize that if he's willing to travel to secondary and tertiary markets, more fans will likely show up. What a compliment to the relationship Troy Coleman has built with his fans that they'd drive 100 miles to see him.

Do you know who your fans are or how far they are willing to travel to see you? Do you know with certainty what they want and how they want to consume that product or service? A short, easy-to-answer online survey can be an excellent first step to learning more about why your clients love you.

Another strategy of Cowboy Troy's you should implement is what management consultant Tom Peters calls "management by walking around." I just call it smart business. Coleman, for example, works the merchandise table at his live shows as often as possible. He doesn't do so out of necessity, as he has a staff member assigned to the task. He chooses to work the merchandise table in order to make a personal connection with his fans. Walking around, signing autographs, and working his own merch table allows him to perform a field audit in each market—in essence conducting a listening tour. Observing what the fans are buying and asking them questions helps him know exactly what they want. It taught him to simplify some of his offerings and to pay attention to the color preferences his fans have for T-shirts, drink koozies, and hats.

It's important you perform your own version of his field audits because a confused mind never buys. By keeping your finger on the pulse of your fans you'll learn their preferences, consumption habits, and how your product or service fits their lifestyle. Remember, if you want better results, you need to start with asking better questions.

Stadium Steps

1. How are you custom tailoring the experience you offer to make it unique and memorable for your customers?
2. When is the ideal time to put a listening tour on your calendar as an annual event?
3. What's the most effective way to differentiate your brand from the competition and avoid the commoditization trap?
4. What are the critical questions you need to ask your fans to better learn their preferences and how they consume your product or service?

CHAPTER 20

Chemistry

In any team sport, the best teams have consistency and chemistry.
—Roger Staubach, NFL Hall of Fame quarterback

You win in the locker room before you win in the stadium. I'm sure at some point you have heard that expression in sports. Clichéd as it may seem, truer words were never spoken—I can tell you from experience. The same holds true in the sport of business. You win in the office first, then in the marketplace.

How do common teams composed of common individuals get uncommon results? Team chemistry. Many organizations make the mistake of believing that all they have to do is stockpile talent to be successful. Talent alone doesn't win.

$$2 + 2 \text{ does } not \text{ equal } 4$$

$$2 + 2 \text{ can equal 3 or } 2 + 2 \text{ can equal 5}$$

Whatever the field—music, business, or sports—the whole is never equal to the sum of its parts. It is either greater than or less than, depending on one thing: team chemistry. It's a little thing that makes a big difference, and it's a little thing that often gets overlooked because it's not easily quantifiable. It's intangible yet powerful, and smart organizations hold team chemistry as priority number one.

Them

"Individually, on paper, we're each misfits, but when you put us together we fit together perfectly." This was Tyrone Carreker's description of the unique team of musicians who make up Sam Hunt's band. Hunt was a college quarterback at University of Alabama, Birmingham, who didn't even learn how to play the guitar until midway through college and who originally pursued an NFL career as a free agent with the Kansas City Chiefs before choosing a career in music. His band members are Tyrone Carreker, a former college basketball player and blues guitarist; Joshua Burkett, a guitarist formerly of a Christian rock band; and drummer Joshua Sales, who moved to Nashville from Indiana with the sole intention of becoming a professional drummer.

The band finished 2015 with country music's top-selling album and two of the top three best-selling songs, with one of the tracks sitting at number one for eleven weeks. Hunt also won New Artist of the Year at the American Music Awards in 2015 and was even nominated for a Grammy.

How do you go from humble beginnings to national prominence in such short order? Spending time together off stage has facilitated the band's growth exponentially. The four band members share a small house in Nashville, and their living situation is very intentional—it allows them to spend more time together, develop synergy, and practice their craft. Carreker explained that when one of them would go to sleep, he'd fall asleep to the sound of his bandmates/housemates practicing their music in the living room. It's no small coincidence that their chemistry on stage is the equivalent of finishing one another's sentences.

You can't put a price tag on the chemistry that develops when you eat together, work out together, and even play pick-up basketball at the local YMCA, as they do. There's a tremendous carryover effect, with that chemistry bleeding into your profession.

When I interviewed Tyrone Carreker, he shared that the fact that both he and Sam were collegiate athletes definitely played a huge role in their musical success. The insights into the value of teamwork, chemistry, and culture they gained as athletes in the stadium served them well as musicians trying to reach stadium status in a new industry. I find it no small coincidence that country music's most successful artists are also former athletes: Garth Brooks, Toby Keith, Kenny Chesney, Chase Rice, Jake Owen, Trace Adkins, and Lee Brice, to name a few.

Bru

Success leaves clues, and as a former college coach I can tell you that the leadership and teamwork and dedication you learn as an athlete serves you well as a professional. It's no small coincidence that the musicians I mentioned earlier are among the brightest stars and they played a team sport.

The sport doesn't have to be football, but team sports have so much to teach. They teach you to be a part of something bigger than yourself and that you cannot have personal success without the help of teammates. This is as true in business as it is in sports. Playing competitive sports can be a very humbling experience, much like working in the business of music or any other business can be humbling. Sports have the ability to break down racial and cultural barriers. When you're on the field, you see your teammates for the skill set and unique abilities each possesses, and not for the color of their skin. You depend on one another and love one another, which is a practice the business world needs to embrace.

I can attest to the fact that the most successful teams I coached weren't necessarily the best "on paper." Rather, they were the teams that lived together in a house off campus or in adjoining suites on campus where they cooked for one another, ate together, tutored one another, and even watched game film together in their free time. These were the teams that gelled on the field exceptionally well. Team chemistry became the X-factor in games where we were outmanned but not outmatched. My NCAA Final Four team in 2002 is a great example: we had a smaller roster and lower budget than everyone in our league, had less scholarship money than our archrivals, and did not have a roster filled with All-Americans, by any stretch. What we did have was a large senior class of players who lived together in on-campus suites for four years, and some of the players had even attended high school together or grown up in the same areas before they arrived at the college. A majority were education majors and were in many of the same classes together. In the off-season they traveled together in the study abroad programs, student-taught in the same elementary schools, and volunteered together on community service projects. They invested a lot of time together off the field, and, as a result, they were a very tightly knit group, which enabled them to maximize their potential on the field. In this equation, two plus two was definitely five, if not more.

On the flipside, the years I had teams with players who belonged to a variety of fraternities, lived apart, and didn't sit together for meals, we struggled on the field—even when we had superior talent with a roster containing multiple All-Americans. If we were lucky two plus two equaled maybe three, at most.

This phenomenon certainly isn't limited to those who perform in stadiums. I see the same thing in corporate America today. One of the largest hospitals in northern New England was a client of mine, and in 2008 the hospital brought me in to do leadership development work with management. A couple of years later, after several budget cuts, they brought me back, only this time for teambuilding with all the departments in one of the satellite buildings on the hospital campus. Silos had developed within each department, and people simply weren't communicating across departments, much less working well with one another.

The full-day training went well, but what was eye-opening was what the feedback from the session revealed. While the employees enjoyed the workshop and found it beneficial, the common theme was that the most valuable part of the experience was eating lunch with colleagues and discussing work-related projects. When I spoke with Susan, the director of organizational development, she explained that in the last round of budget cuts the hospital administration had closed the small cafeteria in the satellite building, and employees were required to go to the main hospital cafeteria to get their lunch. The cafeteria at the satellite building hadn't even prepared the food; they'd simply served the meals delivered from the main cafeteria. Regardless, hospital leadership viewed the satellite cafeteria as an unnecessary luxury, an expense and not an investment.

As a result, many employees packed lunch and ate at their desks, and those who bought lunch actually had a shorter drive to a restaurant off campus than to the cafeteria across campus. Without the opportunity to sit down at lunch and discuss things face to face while breaking bread together, employees' teamwork and communication suffered.

An attempt to save money resulted in an exponentially greater expense, which was lost revenue due to poor communication and a lack of teamwork. There is absolute value in proximity, whether it's your band members all being housemates, your team members living together as roommates, or your employees eating together as teammates. Chemistry doesn't happen by accident, and the most important things may be immeasurable, without a clear-cut ROI in the budget. But those immeasurable things exist nonetheless.

If you're wondering, the hospital never did bring back that small cafeteria, and this serves as a cautionary tale: don't be pennywise and dollar foolish when it comes to investing in your people. The value of the chemistry created among employees gathering in informal spaces is hard to estimate.

Simple is powerful. After I retired from college coaching, I managed the sales team of a group of ESPN Radio stations and deliberately recruited and hired many former team sport athletes because they understood teamwork and chemistry. But I found that if you don't reinforce the idea of teamwork, even a former athlete won't keep it top of mind after his or her playing career is over. To break up the stress of the daily grind and to get people out of the office and energized, I would organize different games. Whether it was throwing a football around and having a tailgate party in the parking lot or playing a Wiffle Ball game in the field behind the office building, we were able to build chemistry and send a subtle but powerful message that gaining and maintaining chemistry was a priority.

You

More important than the raw talent on your roster or the credentials on the individual's resumes at your organization is the chemistry on staff. How do you build chemistry? You coach it by hiring what I call a shade of gray—as in gray hair. A mentor with wisdom and historical perspective can provide great insight.

Take a page out of Coach Urban Meyer's playbook and execute his strategy of hiring success in the form of more mature, more experienced staff. A key ingredient in the success of the University of Florida football program involved that shade of gray. In 2003 former coach Urban Meyer hired Hiram de Fries, a retired lawyer and oil executive, to be the team's chemistry coach. De Fries's job description: to make sure everyone is on the same page, on and off the field. Two National Championships and four conference championships later, Meyer indicates that he thinks de Fries was more important to the Gators' success than anything else. In fact, it was so important that when Meyer left Florida and went to Ohio State University, he had his contract specifically written to allow him to bring one person with him: his chemistry coach Hiram de Fries. Another National Championship showed just how important team chemistry is at the stadium status level.

Clearly, aligning vision with values and strong mentoring are mission critical. As you recruit and construct your team, be on the lookout for your chemistry coach. You should also make a conscious effort to invest in intangibles like eating together and spending time together offsite during and after business hours. Incorporate your employees' families into the activities to create a family environment within your company.

A shining example of someone who works to create strong chemistry among his team is my client Phil Bolduc, CEO of Neokraft Sign Inc., and his team-building idea is one you can easily adapt and use for your business. He and his management team cook and serve his staff breakfast before their Tuesday morning meetings. While it may seem like a simple gesture, the executives exhibit servant leadership and they also make what might otherwise be a run-of-the-mill weekly meeting something the employees look forward to and want to attend. Members from different departments can chat and share ideas during the meal. Some of their best breakthroughs take place during breakfast.

Phil also hosts a weekend-long river rafting and camping trip for employees and their families every summer. The families appreciate the thought that goes into the weekend as well as Phil's investment of time and resources. When your people are working long hours and their jobs involve travel away from home, bringing the families together and saying thank you goes a long way toward recognizing their commitment.

Little things make a big difference and they cannot be underestimated. The intangibles like chemistry, culture, and fit don't just help us excel in business, they are the same qualities that help us excel in life.

Stadium Steps

1. List three ways you can make 2 + 2 = 5 on your team by investing in additional time together.
2. Who will be the Hiram de Fries on your team, and be in charge of keeping everyone on the same page?
3. Teams that play together, stay together. What activities unrelated to work can you organize for your staff to teach and reinforce the concept of team chemistry.

CHAPTER 21

Your Front Row Seats

You aren't wealthy until you have something money can't buy.
—Garth Brooks, American country singer and songwriter

You can learn a lot about getting better at your craft from the masters. Garth Brooks knows he's in the marketing business first and the music business second. (His degree from Oklahoma State is in advertising. He was a marketer long before he was a writer or a singer.) Brooks is a world-class showman and a master at creating unforgettable experiences. If you went to a Garth Brooks concert, you'd see him smash his guitar, use pyrotechnics and fog machines, levitate out of a giant piano, and swing over the crowd on ropes. Brooks is so high energy that his stage crew had to have a mic built into his cowboy hat.

Regardless of the industry you work in, you, too, are in the marketing business first and your chosen profession second. We are all in sales and marketing. We sell and market our ideas for a living; it's what makes the world go round. From a personal standpoint, if there were no marketing you'd have no friends or significant other. You market yourself to people to get them to be friends with you. You market yourself to a person you're attracted to so you can get a date. Professionally, teachers market content to spark a desire to learn in students, salespeople market products, coaches market programs, and consultants market themselves. No matter what you do, if you can't package and sell what you've got, you're in trouble.

Brooks's appeal goes deeper than showmanship and marketing savvy—he knows how to make people feel like a million bucks. Especially the folks who don't have deep pockets.

Them

If you've never been to a Garth Brooks concert, you need to experience him live. You'll get more than a concert—you'll get an education. If you have seen him live, you'll probably be nodding in agreement momentarily—you'll know exactly the feeling I'm about to describe. There's one common theme that emerges every time, regardless of audience size. Whether you are in the balcony or the front row at a Garth Brooks concert, you will feel like he is looking right at you and you're the only one there. He smiles, and you feel he's looking right at you and smiling. I've seen him in a small venue in Pennsylvania and in New York City's Central Park with 250,000 other fans. In Central Park, we arrived late and were at the back of the audience, but we still felt he was looking right at us, almost serenading us. There is a simple but powerful reason Brooks can project this feeling.

Brooks is so dialed in to his customer's perspective that, in every arena he performs in, the morning of the performance he sits up in the back row or in the obstructed-view seat that is the worst in the house. He does this to better understand how his customers see him and how well they see him. The back row customers tend to be some of the most loyal fans at any concert. These are folks who have probably pinched pennies and saved up for months to purchase his tickets. To stay connected with them and others in less desirable seats in the house, Brooks would often fly out on wires to various parts of the arena and perform a song or two to give those folks a taste of the front row seats. During a couple of his tours, he was criticized for his "theatrics in flying all over the arena," and critics thought he did it to feed his ego. They couldn't have been more wrong. Brooks and his fans know the real reason he does it: to surprise, delight, and maintain a connection with his most faithful fans.

To give a few special fans in the back row a true front row experience, at the beginning of his shows Brooks sends security guards to the "nose bleed" seats in the back row. Arena security asks to see the customers' tickets and then explains to them they are sitting in the wrong seats. Right when they begin to get confused or upset because their seats can't get any worse, they're told that they'll be escorted to the correct seats Mr. Brooks has waiting for them . . . in the front row. I saw him do this in the early nineties in Pittsburgh's Mellon Arena and again in 1999.

Brooks used to end his concerts by smashing his guitar on stage for dramatic effect. Then one day he received a letter of complaint from a fan, who told him that it was disrespectful to people who couldn't afford to own a guitar, and if you really want people to explore and learn music, why not give the guitar away during the show instead of smashing it. From that day forward he ended his shows by giving away his guitar.

When I saw him perform in Pennsylvania, a little girl who couldn't have been more than five or six years old was in the front row with her parents, and she handed Garth a rose. In return, Brooks took off his guitar (a Takamine acoustic that retails for $2,079), autographed it with a Sharpie one of his stagehands gave him, and handed it to her. You think that created a once-in-a-lifetime memory for her? And for Brooks, do you think that created a customer for life? Giving back and overdelivering pays dividends. When I saw him perform years later in Central Park, true to form, he again gave his guitar to an adoring fan in the front row.

Nearly twenty years later on his comeback tour he did the same thing in Pittsburgh on February 8, 2015; in Tulsa, Oklahoma, a month earlier, he surprised two young ladies in the crowd by moving them from the back row to the front row.

Bru

You don't have to be a stage entertainer to move fans from the back row to the front row or to build customers for life. You just need to keep your radar on and your antenna up, and look for opportunities to surprise and delight customers in creative ways. Stadium status brands pride themselves on creating personalized and inspired moments throughout the customer experience. They strive to create a culture of warmth and a sense of belonging for all of their fans.

From Idea to Action

During a visit to Nashville in 2001, my wife and I experienced an upgrade similar to those Garth Brooks awards. We purchased tickets to attend the Grand Old Opry on a Saturday night. As we were walking through the courtyard of the Opry on our way to the entrance, we were greeted by two hosts who asked to see our tickets, which were general admission. After noticing where we were seated, they offered us a complimentary upgrade to front row seats. It was too good to be true. They were televising the Opry that night, and we found ourselves on what then was known as TNN, or The Nashville Network. We'd anticipated simply taking in a concert on a Saturday night, but it became the highlight of our entire vacation. And the fact that many years later I still share this story illustrates the value of surprising and delighting your customers in unique and creative ways.

Surprising and delighting your customers is the emotional aspect to the experience, but there's also a practical lesson for all of us in Brooks's genius. When you're speaking or performing in front of a large audience, it's difficult for everyone to hear you. If you've ever spoken in a restaurant, banquet hall, or gymnasium, you know what I mean. There are challenges in every type of environment: room size, audience size, flooring or carpeting, lighting, microphones, sound systems, and audio-visual screens.

In 2015 I gave a keynote speech at a national conference, at Nashville's Gaylord Opryland Convention Center (coincidentally, right next door to the Grand Old Opry). The room was as wide as it was deep, and the back row seemed like it was in another zip code. I wanted to make sure the participants in the back row had the same quality of experience that the folks in the front row had, so I employed Brooks's strategy of sitting in the back row that morning during my walkthrough and sound check for the presentation.

It was fortunate I did that, because, as luck would have it, my mic stopped working in the middle of my talk. I made my way off the stage and walked up the aisle during my speech. I gave the middle and back sections of the convention center front row seats for a little while and asked a couple of audience members in the back row to participate in an activity. This automatically turned the back row into the front row and gave them and their neighbors a front row seat for a portion of the presentation, which I know they appreciated.

This gave me an opportunity to have them introduce themselves by name, and it allowed me to determine how loud I needed to project my voice for the back of the room to hear me for the rest of my speech. Most importantly, by getting the names of a few folks in the back row, I knew I was giving that talk to Melissa, Leslie, and Melanie. My move also allowed the sound technicians (located in the back of the room) to hook me up with a replacement mic and wireless receiver as I was standing right in front of them.

What Does the Back Row Hear?

Sometimes the members of the back row are internal customers, also known as the employees we lead. Depending on their role and vantage point within the organization, they can't see how they are connected to the overall performance of the company. Dr. Stephen Covey, educator and author, did some great research on people from all levels of an organization and their understanding of the company's mission and how their role aligned with the mission. What he found was that six out of eleven people in a company don't understand how their role ties in with the mission of the organization or ties in with the way a product is made and brought to market. Can you imagine that in a team setting? That's the equivalent of six of your players on a team trying to shoot the ball into their own net. That would never happen on a sports team, but it happens every day in corporate America because leadership isn't clear about how individuals in the company contribute to the end result.

In every company, you're going to have people doing menial jobs and you're going to have people doing high-profile, "important" jobs. When I say "important," I mean that the perception is that it is an important job. In reality, if the person welding two pieces of metal together doesn't get it right, the final product is going to have defects and flaws. Every task is dependent on the others. When the shift worker on the assembly line doesn't perform his role well, the success of the end result is going to suffer. Quite simply, everything matters.

Hussey Seating in Berwick, Maine, is a great example of a company that demonstrates just how important everyone's role is. The company manufactures and installs stadium seats, bleachers, and chairs in venues all over North America. If you've ever been in the New England Patriots' stadium in Foxborough, Massachusetts, you've sat in a seat manufactured by Hussey Seating. CEO Tim Hussey hired me to present a teambuilding program to his management team, and in my discussions with Hussey he shared one of the most effective strategies he has used with his team.

A few years ago, Hussey Seating was hired to replace all the seating at the University of New Hampshire's arena. When the project was complete,

Tim closed the plant for an entire day, hired a charter bus, and took every employee in the company to the arena to see the finished installation, sit in the chairs, and have some food, and later that day they watched a game when the arena opened.

Hussey Seating showed the people on its team who perform seemingly menial or repetitive tasks that they're not just welding two pieces of metal together. The company demonstrated in a tangible way how each team member's contribution matters to the finished product. That shift worker isn't just welding a leg onto a seat; he or she is helping to build an arena. The employees all got to sit in the seats they made in the arena they helped build, and to see and feel precisely how the customer experiences their brand, in living color, so to speak.

Some leaders talk about wanting to create alignment between sales, customer service, and manufacturing, and then there are other leaders, like Tim Hussey, who really invest in their people. A significant expense went into closing the entire company for a day: there were the costs of shutting down the production line, as well as those for transporting all the employees by charter bus to another state and feeding them. That's an investment, but it pays dividends because the whole team gets to see how their individual roles contribute to the company's success. I wish more companies would take a page out of Hussey's playbook and show people exactly how their role aligns with the end result.

You

Has it ever occurred to you that your worst customers might want to spend more money with you but they simply can't right now? Don't mistake a small budget for a lack of loyalty—perhaps those customers are giving you all they've got and you just don't know it. By overdelivering and treating your back row customers like front row customers, you guarantee that when the day comes that they have a front-row sort of budget, they will remember how well you treated them even when they didn't have resources.

Do you listen to your customers and fans? Try planting a few undercover fans in your audience to gauge the feedback of your hardworking, paying customers. Have them take notes or mental notes. What are your customers saying? Are they paying attention? What do they love? What were they critical of, and what did they hate? Then discuss the feedback and use the data to make your offering better.

Well before there were television shows like *Undercover Boss*, plenty of savvy leaders rolled up their sleeves and learned what it was like to work on the front lines of their business. When was the last time you performed the jobs of your employees (internal customers) or experienced the company in the same manner they do each day? Have you asked them to describe how their individual role contributes to the organizational goal? Or are you afraid of what you might hear?

The best leaders walk a mile in their customers' shoes and then ensure they overdeliver an experience and connect with customers in a way they simply can't get anywhere else.

Stadium Steps

1. Think about how you, like Garth Brooks, can "give your guitar away" and overdeliver in your business to create customers for life.
2. List three ways you can move some of your customers from "the back row to the front row" to surprise and delight them.
3. Ask yourself: How can I put myself in my customers' shoes and see myself and my business from their vantage point?

CHAPTER 22

Presence

Absence sharpens love, presence strengthens it.
—Thomas Fuller, churchman and historian

There are only two types of people you will meet any place you go: Here I Am's and There You Are's. Which do you think is more interesting? The person who shows up and says, "Here I am!" or the person who shows up and says, "There you are." Suppose we met at an event and we didn't know each other. In our conversation I immediately asked you questions about your interests and abilities. At the end of the event, you'd probably walk out thinking you met someone interesting. I was interesting because I was interested.

Dr. William James, father of the positive psychology movement, said that "the deepest principle in human nature is the craving to be appreciated." When you're interested *in* others, you're interesting *to* others, and they feel appreciated. Being interested is about being truly present in what you're doing.

The one thing world-class performers of all kinds have in common is that they are world-class connectors. They are interesting because they are interested. They are so interested, in fact, that they have amazing presence. Presence is a gift, but not a gift genetically bestowed upon you at birth. It's a gift you give others by caring, paying attention, being mindful, and staying in the moment when you're with them. It's a valuable commodity because it's so darn rare these days. Your presence can go a long way toward elevating you to the big time. And what many don't realize is that you can be big time in a small town.

You expect to find greatness in big cities—it's where the action is. You expect to find the stadium status real estate mogul and Wall Street whiz in New York City or the big-time software and app developer in Silicon Valley. What's even more impressive is finding world-class talent doing big things in small towns.

I found that kind of talent in the small mill town of Lewiston, Maine, during a visit to Bourgeois Guitars. The story of this guitar maker offers a great reminder for all entrepreneurs that your success isn't confined to your city limits and your impact doesn't stop at the state line. Stadium status can be achieved right where you are. You absolutely can take your business to the big time in a small town.

What can an entrepreneur learn from a craftsman? A lot. With that in mind, tune everything else out and invest your undivided attention in what I'm about to share.

My job as a performance coach is to help leaders and their teams consistently perform at a high level and enjoy what they do. So I study world-class talent in an array of industries to see what separates the best from the rest. What you can learn from the best guitar makers in the world very well may change not only the quality of your product but also the quality of your relationships.

Them

As I was touring the Bourgeois manufacturing facility, I was taking photographs, and each time I began to take a photo, my host, Will, made it a point to stop speaking. I told him that was thoughtful but not necessary. He politely told me that what I was doing was important and deserved our full attention.

As we moved from station to station throughout the various areas of the facility, I was introduced to each of the craftsmen. After the first couple of introductions, I picked up on a fascinating pattern. Each did the same thing that Will did. Without fail and with no prompting, each one stopped work to greet me and give me his full attention. The craftsmen all asked questions and showed interest in my work, and they didn't resume their own work until the conversation ended and my questions were answered. When I met with founder Dana Bourgeois and CEO John Karp, wouldn't you know it, they did the same. Bourgeois Guitar has created a culture of mindfulness.

When you make a custom-precision instrument by hand from wood sourced from every corner of the world, you learn to appreciate nuance and pay careful attention to everything and everyone. The company's ability to be truly present and listen to its clients is a big factor in why its client list reads like a who's who of country and bluegrass music and acoustic specialty shops.

When Bourgeois employees are working on the wood, it's the only thing in their world. When they are speaking with someone, that person is the only thing in their world. Imagine how much better your results would be if you took this same approach.

Bru

I have two coaching clients who represent the antithesis of Bourgeois's mindset. A client I'll call "Ted" wakes up at 4 a.m., heads into the office at 4:30, and begins his workday at 5. He ends his "first shift" at 6 p.m., and after dinner begins his second shift until he drifts off to sleep around 11 p.m. Then he does it all again the next day, seven days a week. Ted has put himself into cognitive overload. He's so busy he's forgotten how to be truly present with others and alone with his thoughts.

A second client, I'll call her "Rachel," is a self-proclaimed workaholic. She is busy so she skips lunch, saying she just eats stress for lunch. Rachel sleeps with her BlackBerry on vibrate under her pillow so she doesn't miss any messages or calls from overseas. No surprise, she has trouble getting to sleep, goes through the day fatigued, and often tries to monitor what's happening in her company's manufacturing plant through the window while she's working on her office computer and fielding phone calls.

Both Ted and Rachel are stressed out, and are so connected to their devices that they're disconnected from their employees. As a result, they don't feel like they're doing anything well. I explained that it's simply because their busyness is the enemy of their business. They aren't just trying to do everything, they're trying to do everything all at once. Like having multiple apps open on a smartphone, the multitude of simultaneous tasks are draining their batteries and impairing their performance.

If busyness is the enemy of your business (and it is), then presence is your competitive advantage. In my work as an executive coach, I advise clients to "be where your feet are." What I mean by this is to eliminate distraction, focus on one thing at a time, and be fully present in the moment.

Ted and Rachel are a work in progress, and I've encouraged them to visit Bourgeois to see what being truly present looks like and how it facilitates high performance and world-class craftsmanship.

These luthiers (aka guitar makers) literally are standing at their workstations, feet firmly planted on the ground and pointed in the direction of the piece of wood they are working on. They focus on one thing: being present and delivering the standard of excellence Bourgeois's instruments have become known for worldwide.

Such focus is also what separates the best athletes from the rest. They don't replay the last play in their mind, they focus on the present. Make focus what separates you from your competition.

I had a player on my 2002 NCAA Final Four team, Keith, who was on an absolute tear in our playoff run. In the conference championship semifinal, he scored two goals and an assist in a thirty-three-second span at the end of the first quarter. When he came off the field at the end of the quarter I said to him, "Great job, Keith, three points in thirty-three seconds! What were you thinking out there?" He just looked at me and said, "I wasn't." He didn't know the time left in the quarter, who assisted on his goals, who was guarding him, or what the score of the game was; he was so locked in on performing well that time seemed to stand still for him, the game slowed down, and nothing else mattered. In the sports and entertainment world that feeling is called being in the zone. It's really nothing more than mindfulness, and you can capture that same feeling of high performance in your world.

Quite simply, people who perform at a high level and enjoy what they do all practice mindfulness. Intellectually, most of us realize this, but emotionally, it's hard to make it a daily practice.

You

Before you finish the rest of this chapter I want you to participate in a little activity with me.

1. Stand up.
2. Make sure there's nothing within five feet of your arm's length for your right arm.
3. Hold your right hand out in front of you at the level of your hip, then raise your right arm over your head and then lower it as fast as you can five times.
4. Stop.
5. Now we are going to do it again, only this time I want you to raise your arm slowly from your hip up over your head as you count to ten (the count should start at one at your side, reach five when your arm is parallel to the floor and hit ten when your arm is stretched out as high as you can raise it over your head).
   a. Feel your arm moving slowly through the air at your side.
   b. Feel the material of your shirtsleeve moving across your shoulder and down your arm.
   c. Notice how your deltoid (shoulder) muscle tightens as your arm rises up to shoulder height.
   d. As your arm passes up over your head, feel your serratus and latissimus (back) muscles stretch out as you raise your fingertips as high as you can to the sky.

What was the difference between the first time and the second time you did the exercise? The first time, you were just going through the motions, trying to get done as quickly as possible. There was probably little to no technique involved in your first try. You also probably had very little, if any, awareness of what you and your body were really doing. The second time around, you noticed exactly what you were doing and how you were doing it, and you were not in a hurry. You felt what was going on. You were being where your feet are.

This is the difference between busyness and presence in your performance at work, too. Are you going through the motions or are you truly present in the moment while performing? When you're present, your brain and your body are working together in unison mindfully. It's the difference between just showing up at work and showing up at work with intention and focus.

You're probably more like Ted or Rachel than you are like Keith or the luthiers of Bourgeois Guitar. Most Americans are. I shared these stories to help you realize you're not alone. When I interviewed Jamie Perry, vice president of brand and product development for JetBlue airlines, he revealed that JetBlue commissioned Harris Interactive to conduct a poll of 2,000 Americans. According to the poll results, the vast majority (86 percent) of Americans believe the nation has a "busyness" epidemic. He also revealed that, among those who do, 68 percent indicated that stress causes and/or contributes to this epidemic. We are all running a race, but the question is: are we slowing down enough to enjoy the trip?

The hardest aspect of my job as an executive coach is trying to get CEOs like Ted and Rachel to sit still for twenty minutes a day in quiet, contemplative thought. Ted confided that he couldn't make it five minutes much less twenty, so we dialed it back to thirty seconds.

Do you ever shut everything down and sit still with your thoughts? Have you ever tested how long you can create a distraction-free environment and simply be present in the moment, laser focused on what you are doing?

A great strategy to counter distraction is—when you feel yourself being pulled from the present—to look down at your feet, feel your soles on the ground, and bring your mind back to the present for thirty seconds.

In this age of digital distraction, there is some evidence that humans' attention spans are shorter than they were even a few years ago. How much shorter? Shorter than the attention span of a goldfish, according to some. Seriously. A figure reported by Statistics Brain notes that the human attention span is 8.25 seconds, which is shorter than that of a goldfish (9 seconds). This explains the popularity of Vine videos (maximum length, 6 seconds), emojis (which visually depict an emotion in one character), and tweets (which are 140 characters or fewer), and clarifies why there's a movement to limit e-mails to five sentences in length.

This shortening attention span is why you can't expect employees to focus for hours at a time or clients to sit through a thirty-minute presentation and maintain their undivided attention. Even the best of the best struggle with focus, so much so that New England Patriots head football coach Bill Belichick intentionally only shows his players thirty-second clips of film and communicates important information to them while coaching in thirty-second sound bites. These are more easily consumable and, consequently, more memorable. The thirty-second exercise you are about to experience has become my best practice on how I teach, coach, and relay important concepts when speaking to or training organizations.

The Thirty-Second Sound Bite

To get your body ready for what your mind is about to do, please sit up straight in your seat, put your feet flat on the ground, and place your hands on your thighs. Next, I would like you to read the text in the following box as if you hear my voice speaking the words on the paper directly into your mind.

Our thirty seconds are about to begin: ready, set, go . . .

> For short amounts of time, you can do anything you put your mind to. Your focus, attention, and energy can be directed like a laser beam onto a specific target. The focus you're utilizing right now is different than it was a page ago or even ten seconds ago. Can you feel that?
>
> Right now, you're demonstrating the fact that you have the ability to be precisely where your feet are, present and locked in on the one thing you're supposed to be doing, reading.
>
> Take this technique, carry it off the page, and put it into your work. When you feel yourself getting distracted, just recenter and try to be where your feet are for thirty seconds.

Okay, that was thirty seconds, so you can go ahead and space out again.

Could you feel the difference in the focus and intensity with which you read the contents of the text box? I bet you found yourself able to mentally block out background noises and other environmental distractions during that short time. This is simply a function of very deliberate practice. If I asked you to read for the next hour with that same level of focus you would think I were nuts. We get better at focus the more we practice focusing and refocusing, which is why, like my client Ted, we need to start practicing mindfulness in small increments of time. You can lock in your focus whenever you want on whatever you want, you just need to commit to deliberate practice.

If you've ever been to a concert in a stadium and watched from the upper deck, you'd notice a pattern, one that's easier to see when you have a bird's-eye view. As the musician steps up to the mic, everyone is present and paying attention. During the song, concertgoers have their focus locked in, and many are even singing along. Then, when the song ends, the audience's focus shifts away temporarily. I would argue that the performers do the same. There is a focus and then a shift, then another period of focus and a shift, and the pattern repeats itself. Your work environment is no different. Your presence and focus are choices, and they can be practiced and refined.

The more we multitask, the less effective we are, because we send our brain into overload and it can't process two things at once.

The team at Bourgeois isn't just present with their guests; I observed them doing the same thing with one another. And I came to learn that they do the same with their retailers and musicians. Bourgeois is an industry leader in high-end custom acoustic guitars. How can such a small company rise to this position? The management and craftspeople at Bourgeois Guitars have made being where their feet are a best practice; it's what makes them world-class craftsmen. You can do the exact same thing in your business. Be where your feet are and give people the gift of your presence. It's the most valuable gift you can give.

Stadium Steps to World Class Focus

1. Create tech-free zones (TFZs). Ban devices in your meetings. Besides eliminating distractions and encouraging eye contact and concentration, this policy will significantly shorten the length of your meetings and increase participation and productivity.
2. Institute tech-free time (TFT). When meeting with employees, customers, or colleagues, close your laptop, and don't answer your phone or respond to texts. Taking care of other business while you are in a conversation devalues and disrespects the person who approached you.
3. "There You Are": treat each person you come in contact with like he or she is the most important person in the world, or at least your world.
4. Be where your feet are. Listen to what's not being said as much as what is being said.

CHAPTER 23

Yours versus Theirs

Don't compare your preseason to someone else's postseason.
—Coach Morgan Randall, great American
philosopher and coaching legend

I enjoy horseback riding, and I take my kids to the barn each weekend to ride. One week, my daughter Julia was studying the animal kingdom in school and that Saturday at the barn she shared an expression she learned in school: "Eyes on the front, born to hunt; eyes on the side, born to hide." This rhyme helps differentiate predators from prey. Tigers, for example, have eyes in the front of their heads and are hunters, while horses have eyes on the side of their heads and tend to be prey. The expression is also an apt metaphor for the way we approach our work.

With eyes on the sides of their heads, horses obviously have great peripheral vision, and in the wild that feature serves them well for survival purposes. For racehorses, though, such vision is detrimental, and these horses can end up running off course unless they are made to remain on track. This is why trainers place blinders on racehorses' bridles—they don't want the horses to be distracted by what's next to or behind them. The blinders keep racehorses focused on what's in front of them.

Like a racehorse, you are an athlete. You're training and competing every day. Competitors are prone to comparison, the ultimate performance killer. Comparison equals self-sabotage, because it takes our eyes off the prize and we run off course. In fact, comparison is perhaps the most dangerous activity we engage in, personally and professionally. Yet we all compare ourselves to others in some way; it's human nature. Comparison is also a thief. It robs us of our self-confidence and, in the process, steals our peace of mind.

We are all performers and should equip ourselves with a set of "entrepreneurial blinders" to help us avoid the trap of comparison. We have to get to the point where we run our race against no one but ourselves. In that kind of race, giving a full effort and playing all out is more important than beating others.

If you're comparing yourself to whoever is running neck and neck with you or who might be catching up, you won't succeed because you have divided your attention. Would you want your surgeon, while performing open-heart surgery, to compare his incisions to those of his colleague performing the same procedure an operating table away? Comparison doesn't serve anyone well because it rarely offers an accurate measurement. A pair of my clients demonstrate how virtually all comparison is apples to oranges, as the saying goes.

Them

A few years ago I had two college head coaches as clients (even coaches need coaches). Out of respect for their privacy, I've left out their names and the sport they coach. Neither one knew the other personally, nor did either coach know the other was also a client. The two have much in common, as they are about the same age and are both husbands and fathers. One was a highly successful Division One coach, in his prime and at the pinnacle of his profession. He's very well compensated financially, his career has been filled with championships and professional accolades, and he's a media darling. In short, there's no question that a lot of coaches want to grow up to be just like him someday.

My other client, a coach at a small college, had a career that would be described by most in the coaching profession as fairly successful. He wasn't winning any national championships, and you'd never see him on ESPN, but he has built a successful program, his players graduate, and he's done everything the right way.

In my work with these clients, I learned just how miserable both were in their situations. The high-profile Division One coach wished he wasn't always on the road and away from his family. He was frustrated by the unrelenting external (and internal) pressure to win, the time commitment, and the political dealings with boosters and alumni. He was literally making himself physically and emotionally sick.

The small college coach was equally frustrated, but his frustrations were of a different character. He was playing the comparison game, convinced he'd be happy someday when he landed a Division One coaching job. He explained that if he was making "Division One money" his problems would go away; he'd have the budget he needed to be successful and he'd have a sizable staff to help carry the workload. He wished the alumni and boosters at his small college cared enough to actually be involved in the program instead of being absent. Life for him consisted of frequent anxiety attacks and trouble sleeping most nights.

During a coaching session, my Division One client explained to me that he was jealous of small college coaches. They had more job security, less travel, less pressure to win, and less media scrutiny, and could enjoy their relative anonymity in their respective communities. He also commented that he often felt the money he was making wasn't worth the headaches that came with the job at the Division One level. He even mentioned my other client by name as a coach who has the kind of career he wished he had! Talk about irony.

The problem my small college client was having is that he was comparing his blooper reel to the highlight reel of one of his professional peers. Sadly, it didn't matter what he achieved because, in comparing his blooper reel to someone else's highlight reel, he'd never measure up. And he had no idea what was going on behind the scenes at the next level he was comparing himself to.

Are you comparing your blooper reel to someone else's highlight reel? I know I've been guilty of doing just that. And, as you're about to learn, the grass isn't always greener.

Bru

My next-door neighbor, Bill, is one of the top Realtors in the state, and when you walk past his property you can tell he's elevated curb appeal to an art form. His front yard is so green you'd think it was artificial turf, and his landscaping looks like something you'd see on HGTV. Bill's lawn is so picture perfect, I half expect to see him edging his driveway with nail clippers when I take my daily walk past his house with our dog. And when I walk by, believe me, I'm looking at it with envy. As we would make the turn for home I often found myself in a bad mood or feeling inferior when I unleashed the dog in our back yard. Mainly, because I would look at our yard and see bare patches (and some dog poop) and my kids' bikes and toys scattered all over, along with the usual branches and leaves. Not exactly HGTV material.

Then one day I got a text from Bill telling me that his family was going to be away on vacation for the week and wanting to know if I'd be willing to bring his garbage cans in from the curb so they didn't sit out all week and give the appearance no one was home. I agreed, and for my own mental health, I am forever glad that I did. When I brought his garbage cans around to the back of his house I was shocked. I saw bare patches of dirt (and some dog poop), overturned lawn chairs, his kids' bikes and toys scattered all over, and piles of unstacked firewood and leaves.

Like a brick to the head, it hit me: I'd been comparing his front yard to my back yard and in the process I was making myself feel inferior. Then it hit me like a cinderblock to the head that we often do the same thing with our businesses. We compare our backstage to our competition's center stage.

There's a big difference between center stage and backstage, whether the performance is a concert, a play, a show, or a game under the lights in the stadium. The same holds true in your industry and at your place of business. What you never want to do is compare your backstage to other people's center stage. Comparison is the ultimate performance killer. What you see back stage or behind the scenes is always a lot messier; it's at best controlled chaos. This is the case for everyone, big stars and budding stars. Everyone has this same backstage situation in their business, regardless of the level of fame they've attained.

Think about the Grand Old Opry; when the music rolls, the curtain is pulled up, and the show begins, everyone is in the right place and all are dressed to perfection on center stage. What you don't see is that backstage, in the last few minutes before the show starts, it's a madhouse. Some people forget things, others are behind schedule, and a few more have some sort of wardrobe or equipment malfunction no one could have anticipated.

You

It's very easy to compare your business to others—too easy. The problem is that you're making a false comparison. You're comparing your knowledge of what happens backstage in your business to what's going on center stage in others' businesses. You don't get to peek behind their curtain. It's unfortunate, too, because what you would find is a lot of the same chaos and mayhem your business experiences. You think the others appear to be consummate professionals all the time, and it looks so easy. The fact is, everyone has the same challenges, but you only get to see your backstage, not theirs.

Today's era of Photoshop, airbrushing, spray-on tans, and video editing makes people feel inferior because all that's visible is the stars' center stage. Meanwhile, those stars have got the same issues everyone else faces and, in some cases, more.

Comparison is also a thief because everybody exaggerates—not just in person but also on social media and on the web. People routinely embellish sales numbers and their income, post only the highlights and positives from their life on Facebook, and many will even buy followers on social media to give the illusion of greater fame and popularity. Certain politicians and celebrities come to mind. This is not a political commentary or an indictment of Hollywood; it's to illustrate the fact that if high-profile politicians and celebrities do it, people in your industry likely are too. Everybody exaggerates, so don't compare—you'll waste so much time comparing that you find you're not actually producing.

The way you advance your career or business from backstage to center stage isn't by comparing yourself to the competition; it's by realizing who the true competition really is. The only true comparison is between who you are today and who you were yesterday. Focus on being better today than you were yesterday and better tomorrow than you are today.

Make the best of what you've got where you are while you are there. This is the only surefire, proven way to outgrow the stage you are on and advance your career. Top performers didn't land at the top of the charts by accident; they created their own opportunities. Excellence in all things is achieved through excellence in small things. The stars advanced to center stage because they were willing to deliver excellence in small things. There will always be a certain number of people who are born on third base and think they hit a triple, but that type of success, if we can even call it that, is rarely sustained because they didn't earn it.

Remember, everybody starts off nowhere and only through hard work, persistence, and a little luck do they get somewhere. Nobody starts off at the top.

Overnight success is thousands of nights in the making, and only by doing the work and putting in the time do people advance to center stage in their industry.

Maybe your stage is smaller than what you want it to be; so what? The only way to outgrow it is to keep your eyes on what's in front of you and put in the real work. Chase your dreams, not your competition, because the only accurate measurement is progress, not perfection.

How often do you look at someone else and assume he's got it good? By playing the comparison game, you're engaging in a no-win game and creating an impossible standard to live up to. All comparisons are apples to oranges. Can you recalibrate your perspective to view yourself as already successful at what truly matters?

Comparison places the focus on the wrong person. When you compare, you immediately begin focusing on things you cannot control. You can't control others any more than you control the weather, and trying to do it is a no-win proposition. Ultimately, it's up to us to stop comparing our backstage to our competitors' or colleagues' center stage. How do you stop comparing? By being vigilant about maintaining the proper perspective. Celebrate others' successes and celebrate your own.

I have one trophy that sits on the bookshelf in my office; it's the NCAA semifinalist replica trophy that all players and coaches who competed in the NCAA Final Four (and lost) received. For years, I was haunted by the fact that I'd never won a National Championship and several of my rivals had. Then I realized just how unhealthy the comparison was. They weren't my rivals, they were my friends and colleagues, and I'm happy for them that they reached the pinnacle of our profession. When I look back at the resources at our disposal compared with the resources they had, it was something of a miracle we made it as far as we did. I fell into the comparison trap and had been making an apples-to-oranges comparison when, in reality, our team collectively maximized our potential, which is the only true measure.

Please remember that you don't have to "win the big one" at the highest level to be a champion in your profession. (Trust me, many who do don't feel fulfilled afterward.) If you're not enough without a championship, you'll never be enough with one.

Stadium Steps

1. Keep a daily gratitude journal. When you begin to compare yourself to others, redirect your energy to focus on gratitude. Upward comparison focuses your attention on deficiencies, but gratitude reorients your thinking to what is good. It is impossible for your mind to hold two emotions or thoughts at once. Therefore, focus on what you're grateful for; those things can't be obscured by comparisons to someone who appears to have more or be better. (Key word = appears)

2. Celebrate and document your daily successes in your journal. The only fair and accurate comparison is between who you are today and who you were yesterday. Focus on being better today than you were yesterday and better tomorrow than you are today. Remember, it's about progress, not perfection.

3. Put your blinders on. You can't control what others are doing or how they do it. Make a list of the things in your environment that are within your control, focus exclusively on them, and watch your results soar.

CONCLUSION

The Secret Location of Stadium Status

A person often meets his destiny on the road he took to avoid it.
— Jean de la Fontaine, French poet

My first coaching job was in 1993, when I coached a middle school youth lacrosse team, and my last coaching job was in 2004, when I coached a nationally ranked college lacrosse program to an NCAA Final Four appearance. The opportunity to work my way up in the profession and travel around the country for more than a decade gave me a unique perspective. I learned that coaching in front of 10,000 fans in a packed stadium in the NCAA Championships, with a television camera and microphone shoved in your face during every time out, is no different from coaching in front of ten fans in a county park. Regardless of the level you are on, it feels just as great when you win and hurts every bit as much when you lose.

Stadium status is a state of mind, not a destination. You can make stadium status where you are right now. The number of fans changes, but the game doesn't and neither does your self-worth.

Many entrepreneurs dedicate their entire lives to striving for stadium status. They are being told where stadium status is in their industry and how to get there by self-proclaimed "industry experts." They chase the dream and create the proverbial window dressings that make them appear to be stadium status, only to find themselves discouraged, disappointed, and completely unfulfilled at the end of the day. There are still other entrepreneurs who don't believe they ever had a shot at achieving stadium status, so they run their businesses and lead their lives in quiet desperation, simply wondering what might have been.

Stadium status is the ultimate paradox and, like any mystery, there is one linchpin clue that, once discovered, renders the picture clear and complete. Once you understand the reality surrounding this one clue, you can apply it to your personal and professional life. When you do this, then and only then will amazing things unfold. You will have more job satisfaction and more growth, and will perform at a level you never knew you were capable of. The result of all this is greater clarity, confidence, and direction.

I believe this one thought, this one concept, can change your life and maximize your success:

Stadium status isn't something you achieve, it's someone you become.

Stadium status isn't really a destination, it's a state of the mind. Wherever you are, you're already at stadium status. If you think stadium status refers merely to performing in the biggest venues, in front of the largest crowds, you have fallen into the trap of thinking it's a destination. In reality, stadium status is a journey, and wherever you are on the journey is stadium status.

When you place your focus on your own performance rather than the competition, you will achieve and compete at a higher level. When you play the comparison game and constantly try to measure yourself up to the competition, you're hurting your results.

The reward is not in reaching the stadium. The reward is the road to the stadium.

The absolute value of embracing the stadium status mindset is that you will not only perform at a higher level but you'll also be more fulfilled in the process. Enjoy the journey.

Stadium Status Resources

Visit www.StadiumStatusBook.com to

- Print Stadium Status posters
- Share the Stadium Status Principles with your team and organization
- Download the Stadium Status playlist and other leadership resources
- Watch Stadium Status videos
- Attend a Stadium Status seminar
- Enroll in Coach Bru's Stadium Status coaching program.

Build a Stadium
Status Organization

If you're interested in a custom-tailored keynote speech or training program for your organization based on the Stadium Status principles, contact Coach Bru at:

Phone: (207) 576–9853
E-mail: john@coachbru.com
Online: www.CoachBru.com
Sign up for John's free weekly newsletter at www.CoachBru.com

To purchase bulk copies of *Stadium Status* for large groups or your organization at a discount, please contact your favorite bookseller or Taylor and Francis Publishing (www.routledge.com).

Also by John Brubaker

Figure R-1 *Book cover*, The Secret Playbook

"Shocking and provocative, John Brubaker and Coach Morgan Randall have inspired me to look at old problems with a fresh set of eyes."
—Jeff Squires, President, Prince Edward Island Brewing Co.

Available for purchase at: CoachBru.com

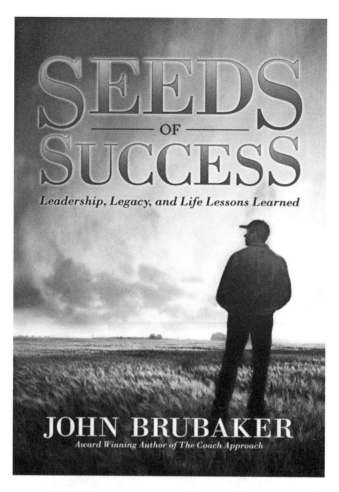

Figure R-2 *Book cover*, Seeds of Success

"Coach Bru has created another slam dunk with *Seeds of Success*. It's a fabulous book with a powerful message. Anyone who reads this will develop a better sense of what it takes to be a leader of significance in life's journey instead of simply chasing success."

Paul Biancardi, National Recruiting Director, ESPN

Available for purchase at: CoachBru.com

Figure R-3 *Book cover*, The Coach Approach

"John shares practical insights from his coaching career to teach you how to lead with your mind and your heart. *The Coach Approach* will teach you winning strategies to bring about game-changing performance in business and life."
—Jon Gordon, *Wall Street Journal* best-selling author of *The Energy Bus* and *Training Camp*

Available for purchase at: CoachBru.com

Index

About the Author

Figure R-4 *John Brubaker*

John Brubaker is a nationally renowned performance consultant, speaker, and author. More importantly, he's a husband and father. John teaches audiences how to achieve stadium status results in business with straightforward tools that turbocharge performance.

Brubaker is the author of numerous books, including Hollywood Book Festival award–winner *Seeds of Success*, *The Secret Playbook of Coach Morgan Randall, The Daily Game Plan,* and *The Coach Approach.* In 2016, his book *Seeds of Success* was adapted into a screenplay for a major motion picture.

Coach Bru has been featured on Fox Sports, ESPN Radio, CBS Radio, and NBC News, as well as in *Forbes, Entrepreneur,* and numerous other media outlets. His principles and strategies are impacting professional sports teams, corporations, universities, and associations. CEOs, entrepreneurs, and coaches call on Coach Bru to motivate their people. Brubaker also coaches some of the world's top executives, coaches, and athletes, helping them perform their best when it matters most.

John Brubaker graduated from Fairleigh Dickinson University with a bachelor's degree in psychology, and he also earned a master's degree in personnel psychology from FDU. He has completed his doctoral coursework in sport psychology at Temple University. For more information visit:

www.CoachBru.com